D1499335

SCAPA

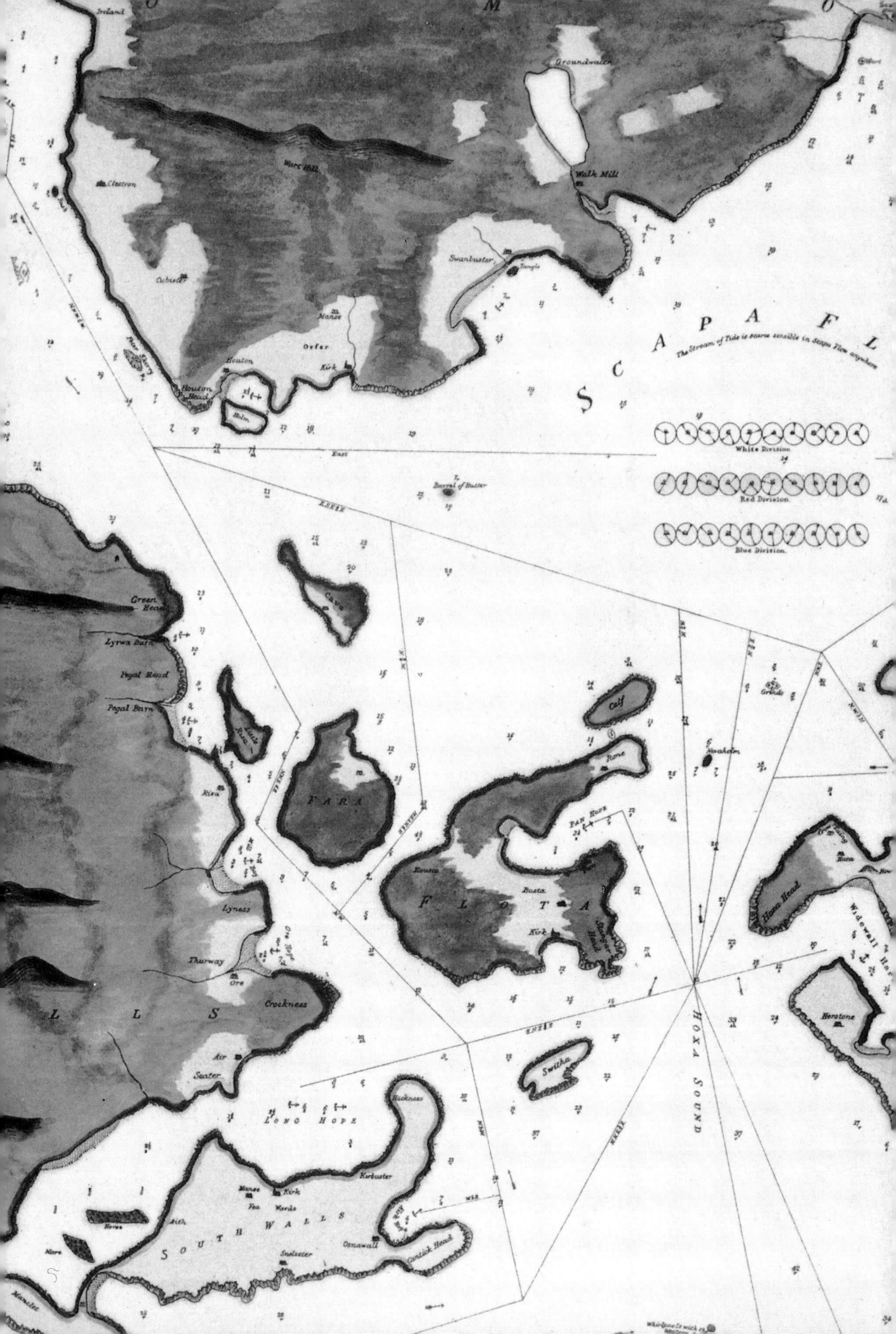
Ireland
Clestron
Ward Hill
Groundwater
Walk Mill
Swanbuster
Cubister
Manse
Orfer
Kirk
Houton
Houton Head
Holm
SCAPA FL
The Stream of Tide is scarce sensible in Scapa Flow anywhere
East
Barrel of Butter
White Division
Red Division
Blue Division
Green Head
Lyrwa Burn
Pegal Head
Pegal Burn
Cava
Calf
Rine
Swahelm
Grinds
FARA
Rise
Pan Hope
FLOTA
Busta
Kirk
Lyness
Thurway
Ore
Ore Hope
Crockness
Air
Seater
Switha
HOXA SOUND
Hoxa Head
Widewall
Herstone
LONG HOPE
Hackness
Kirbuster
Manse
Kirk
Fea
Wards
Aith
SOUTH WALLS
Osmawall
Cantick Head
Snelsetter
Hoxa

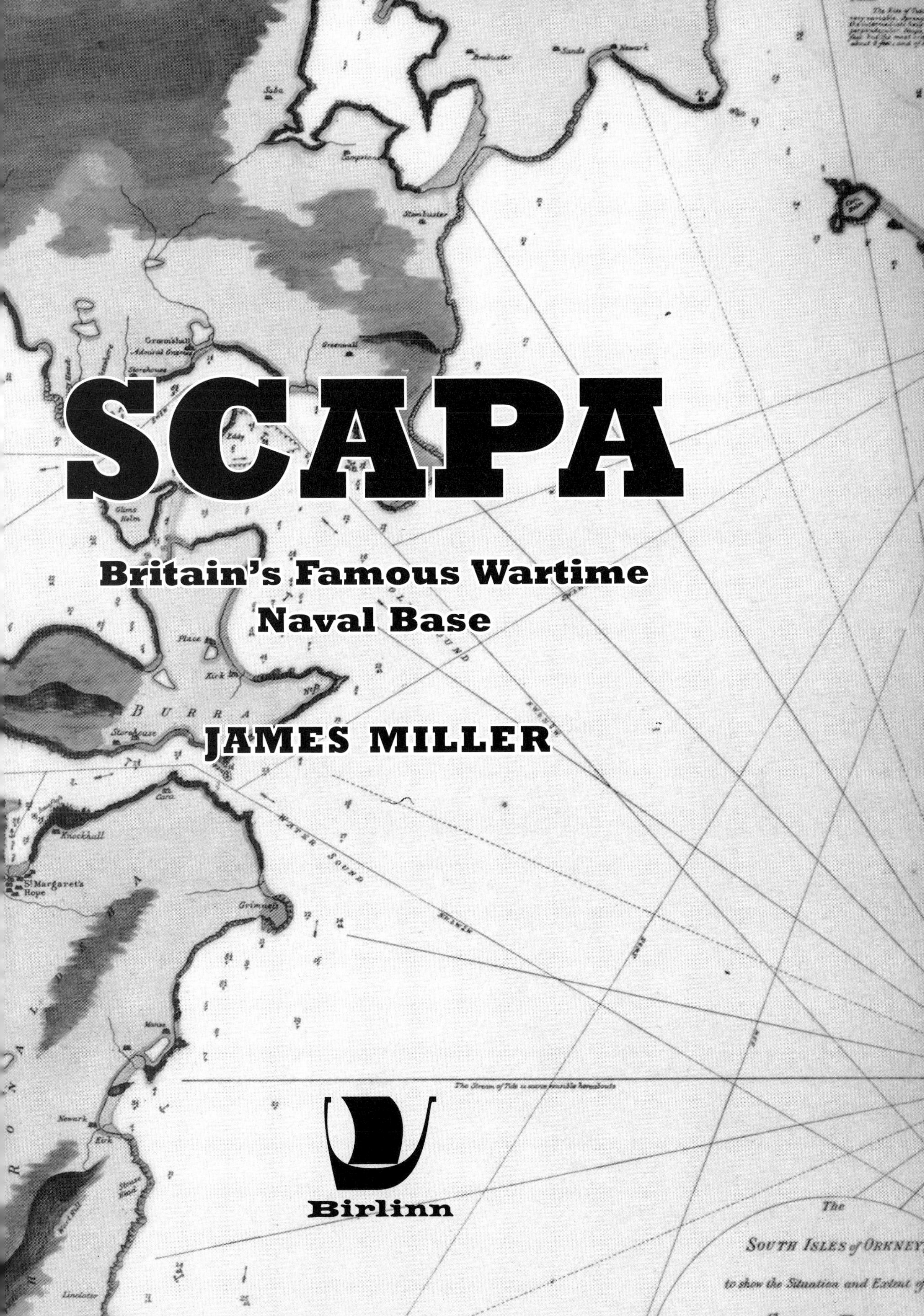

SCAPA

Britain's Famous Wartime Naval Base

JAMES MILLER

Birlinn

Fig. 1
Graeme Spence's map of Scapa Flow, 1812.

First published in 2000 by
Birlinn Limited
8 Canongate Venture
5 New Street
Edinburgh
EH8 8BH

ISBN 1 84158 005 8

British Library Cataloguing-in-Publication Data
A catalogue record for this book is available from the British Library

Text design by James Hutcheson
Typeset by Patty Rennie Production, Stonehaven

Printed and bound by The Bath Press, Bath

ACKNOWLEDGEMENTS

To condense the story of Scapa Flow, already the subject of several books, into one short volume would have been an impossible task without the generous help of many people, including the staff of the public libraries in Kirkwall and Inverness, Lyness Visitor Centre, Stromness Museum, Orkney Wireless Museum, the Imperial War Museum and the Public Record Office, Kew. I owe grateful thanks to several individuals for giving information and sharing memories with me: in Caithness, Mr A. Budge, Noel Donaldson, Sutherland Manson, Brenda Lees and Trudi Mann (Northern Archive, Wick), and Nancy Houston; in Inverness-shire, Geoffrey Davies, Jackie Fanning and John Walling; in Orkney, Ella Stephen, William Mowatt and John Muir; and in Skye, Vice-Admiral Sir Roderick 'Roddy' Macdonald. David Mackie of the Orkney Library Photographic Archive gave generous access to his collection of pictures; and I am extremely grateful to John Walling for permission to use several unique pictures from his father's collection. Once again, I am grateful to Dick Rayner for photographic services and to Duncan McAra for his continuing help and encouragement.

ILLUSTRATION CREDITS

I am grateful to the following sources for permission to use illustrations: A. Budge for Fig. 71; the Imperial War Museum for Figs. 7, 8, 24, 26, 29, 31, 32, 34, 46, 64, 91, 99, 102, 112, 113 and 132; the National Maritime Museum for Fig. 1; Orkney Public Library for Figs. 2, 3, 4, 5, 6, 9, 12, 13, 14, 16, 19, 25, 30, 33, 35, 36, 37, 38, 39, 40, 41, 42, 43, 45, 47, 48, 49, 50, 51, 52, 53, 54, 55, 56, 58, 59, 62, 63, 66, 68, 72, 73, 75, 76, 77, 78, 79, 80, 84, 85, 86, 87, 88, 90, 93, 97, 100, 105, 106, 109, 110, 114, 115, 119, 122, 123, 124, 125, 126, 127, 128, 129, 130 and 131; Orkney Public Library and the Gregor Lamb Collection for Figs. 17, 18, 61, 65, 74, 81, 82, 94, 95, 96, 98, 101, 103, 104, 107, 108, 111, 116, 117, 118 and 120; the Public Record Office, Kew, for Figs. 44, 67, 69, 70 and 83; Vice-Admiral Sir Roderick Macdonald for Figs. 57 and 92; the Royal Commission on Ancient and Historical Monuments of Scotland for Figs. 60 and 121; and John Walling for Figs. 10, 11, 15, 20, 21, 22, 23, 27 and 28. The pictures obtained from the Imperial War Museum, the National Maritime Museum, the Public Record Office and the RCAHMS are Crown Copyright.

The North Sea and the relative positions of British and German bases in both World Wars.

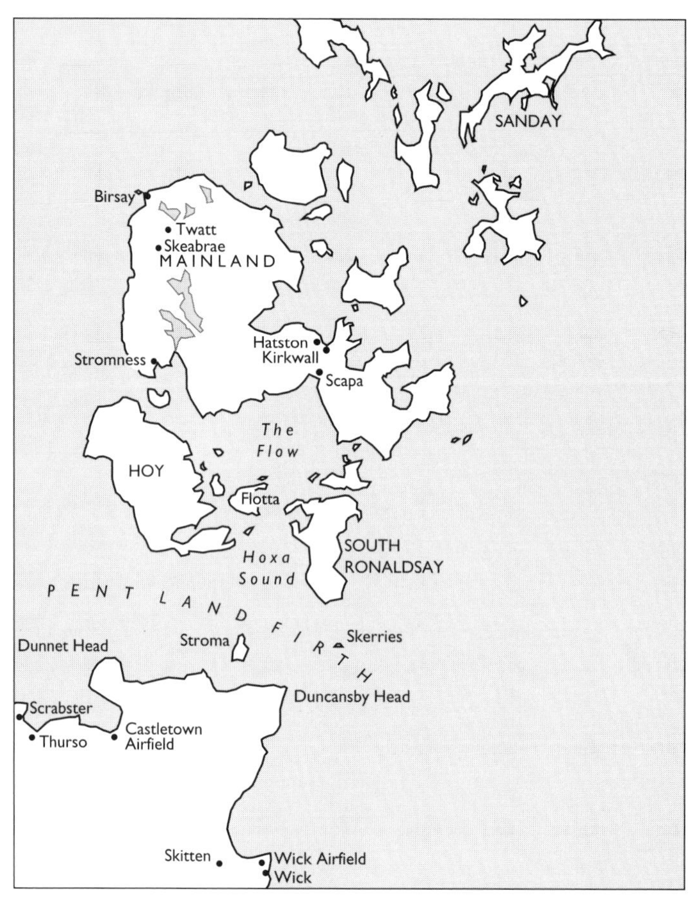

The Pentland Firth and Scapa Flow

SCAPA

James Miller

One summer morning in 1992, I found a piece of broken china lying among the stones and sea-drift at the head of the beach at Aith Hope. On its side was stamped in brown the crest of the Navy, Army and Air Force Institute, a body better known by its initials – NAAFI. There was a motto: *servitor servientium*, 'servant of those who serve'; the piece had obviously come from a mug, a heavy, white mug. It should have been no surprise to fiand it. Aith Hope lies at the junction between the islands of Hoy and South Walls, at the south-west corner of Scapa Flow. The marks left by the former presence of the main base of Britain's Home Fleet are on every hand but somehow this shard of a NAAFI mug, redolent of the strong char beloved by the serviceman, spoke more eloquently of the coming and going of thousands than all the abandoned gun platforms and larger pieces of militaria.

I write thousands advisedly. During the First World War, when the battleships of the Royal Navy swung at anchor in the Flow, the number of naval personnel in Orkney at times reached 100,000. In the Second World War, the influx of servicemen and women pushed the islands' population to 60,000, three times its peacetime size. As well as the crews and shore-based staffs of the navy there were airmen and soldiers from most of the nations fighting under the banner of the Allies; and a posting from the gentler environs of southern England, the home of most of the service personnel, to the stark surrounds of the Flow even gave rise to a rhyming slang phrase 'scapa flow', a variant on scarper, meaning to go away, or disappear for parts unknown. It was here that naval aviation took a crucial step forward, that the largest scuttling of a fleet occurred, that the largest maritime salvage operation took place. It is little wonder the name was erected in the popular mind to join El Alamein, Normandy, Anzio and Burma as places associated with war and became a byword for the remote – Addu Atoll, now Gan, a Royal Navy base in the Indian Ocean, was nicknamed 'Scapa Flow with bloody palm trees'.

An expansive, enclosed basin of sea, some ten miles from east to west, and a similar distance from north to south, the Flow is entirely surrounded by islands. The high bulk of Hoy comprises the western side; the smaller, lower islands of

South Walls, Fara and Flotta lie to the south, with, in the east, South Ronaldsay and Burray, and a scattering of smaller islets and holms. The northern and north-eastern shores of the Flow belong to the mainland of Orkney. Although the frequent gales can whip up an angry sea within the anchorage, the ring of land guarantees shelter from the fiercest weather; and the water in the Flow is deep enough – from twenty to thirty fathoms – to float the largest ships safely.

The main entrance to the Flow is Hoxa Sound between Flotta and South Ronaldsay. This was the gate through which the capital ships came and went; destroyers and smaller craft used the gap called Switha Sound just to the west. Another major entrance to the Flow, Hoy Sound, was less used by naval vessels; it lies in the north-west corner between Hoy and Stromness. The island of Graemsay sits in the middle of the channel here and separates Hoy Sound from the Bring Deeps. On the east side, narrow, comparatively shallow channels used to wend between the islands to connect the Flow to the North Sea; these were all sealed in the Second World War by the construction of the series of causeways still known as the Churchill Barriers.

At the beginning of this century, in a hangover from earlier wars, British naval bases were concentrated in the south of England facing the old enemy: France. The emergence of Germany as a naval power, under Kaiser Wilhelm II, changed this pattern. The development and rapid growth of European navies in the twenty years or so before 1914 has been analysed and described many times.[1] This maritime arms race crystallised by 1912 into a contest between Britain and Germany, but France, Italy, Austro-Hungary, Russia and others also had an interest in dreadnoughts, submarines, torpedoes and the other new aspects of seapower. It was obvious to strategic experts that, in the event of hostilities, the North Sea would become a major theatre. In 1912, some officials in the Admiralty were even worried that courtesy visits to Shetland by German warships might erode the islanders' 'sense of British nationality'; the Orcadians were felt to be less susceptible to enemy influence.[2] In 1903, Rosyth had been designated as a major base, and Cromarty was also made a base but with no anti-submarine protection.

Scapa Flow's potential as a base had been first formally brought to the attention of the Admiralty as long ago as 1812, by Graeme Spence. The latter was the nephew of Murdoch Mackenzie, the first man to map the Flow and its surroundings by the then modern technique of triangulation. Mackenzie's atlas of northern waters had been published in 1750 and had opened the way to greater use of the Pentland Firth by sailing vessels; hitherto they had tended to avoid the dangerous passage. Spence, himself a maritime surveyor for the Admiralty, sent a carefully drawn chart of Scapa Flow to their Lordships along with his 'Proposal for establishing a Temporary Rendezvous for Line-of-Battle

Ships, in a Natural Roadsted [sic] called Scapa Flow, formed by the South Isles of Orkney . . .'.[3]

Spence argued that Scapa Flow was the finest roadstead after Spithead for line-of-battle ships and anticipated the critics of his plan by pointing out that local seamen 'would think light of' the alleged dangers of navigation in the area. On the scale of two inches to the British mile, and coloured in green, brown, yellow and red, his chart is an object of beauty. It failed, however, to convince the Commissioners of the Admiralty to take any action: a note dated 7 July 1812 instructed a clerk to thank Spence for his draft – and that was all.[4]

But not quite all. During the Napoleonic Wars, the Royal Navy found itself with increased business in the north, both in recruiting and in combating the menace of privateers. The latter, mainly French and later American, attacked merchantmen of all types, seizing cargoes and ships, and posed a serious threat to the Baltic trade, a major source of timber, vital to Britain. A convoy system was introduced for merchant ships, with the assembly point in Longhope. Two Martello towers, at Crockness and Hackness, were built to guard the entrances to the anchorage but they were not finished until December 1814 when peace was signed with the Americans and Napoleon was on the verge of defeat.[5]

Fig. 2 (overleaf) *The Royal Navy in Scapa Flow before the First World War.*

Throughout the nineteenth century, Scapa Flow saw little naval activity, apart from surveying parties updating and enlarging upon the earlier charts of Mackenzie and Spence. HMS *Triton* was engaged on this work in 1909, when the Royal Navy began to make use of Scapa Flow in a big way. Ships of the Channel Fleet had paid the occasional visit to Kirkwall Bay – for example in 1898 to show the flag and indulge in public duties – but now the activity was on an altogether grander scale. In April 1909 Orkney was looking forward eagerly to welcoming the visit of the combined Atlantic and Home Fleets. *The Orcadian* published the news that the Fleets would arrive on Saturday the seventeenth and stay until the following Wednesday. Traders made ready to supply the ships with a daily requirement of eighty tons of vegetables and 5,000 loaves. One hundred and thirty cattle had been purchased in the North Isles and the slaughterhouse in Kirkwall went on overtime to cope with the demand for its services. A procession of coal steamers arrived.[6]

At around ten-thirty on the morning of the seventeenth the ships of the navy came out of the haze in the Pentland Firth and passed through Hoxa Sound into the Flow to form a line of twenty-eight battleships and cruisers, 'a most imposing appearance' in the words of *The Orcadian*'s reporter. With their attendant flocks of destroyers, the whole fleet numbered eighty-two vessels. The cold southerly wind did not deter the townsfolk of Kirkwall from flocking out to see this manifestation of Britain's naval might; pleasure trips were organised to

HOME FLEET AT SCAPA FL

ORKNEY. T.K.

view the Fleets on Sunday, and the provost and town officers welcomed the navy and declared that the town's Bignold Park and golf course were open to the men. The Home Fleet was under the command of Admiral Sir William H. May, who flew his flag in HMS *Dreadnought*, and the Atlantic Fleet was led by Vice-Admiral Prince Louis Alexander of Battenberg on HMS *Prince of Wales*.

The people of Flotta had perhaps the best view of the ships as they ringed the island in the Flow. *The Orcadian*'s correspondent there wrote of them 'steadily, grandly, unitedly stemming the racing ebb tide of the Pentland Firth' and wished that the Kaiser could have been there – perhaps he would have then thought twice about competing for naval supremacy.

The Royal Navy returned with a fleet of ninety ships in 1910. By this time considerable pressure was being put on the Liberal government of Herbert Asquith to make Scapa Flow a permanent base. Matters were given more urgency when Winston Churchill was appointed First Sea Lord at the end of 1911. In February 1912, the Admiralty became concerned over the War Office intention to disband the Orkney Territorial Royal Garrison Artillery (TA) forces and asked the Home Ports Defence Committee to consider strengthening Scapa Flow and the Cromarty Firth against torpedo attack. A contingent of seven senior military officers, including the Director of Fortifications and Works and the Director of Artillery, travelled to Wick in March, where they were met and taken to Scapa by HMS *Blonde* on an inspection.[7]

During naval manoeuvres in the summer of 1912, the Royal Marines carried out a defensive exercise on Flotta. On the afternoon of 12 July, they landed in Kirk Bay and by the evening of the following day had placed all their search-lights and had wrestled five of their eight four-inch guns across the peaty ground to strategic positions at Scatwick and Stanger Head to guard the entrances to the Flow. It was reckoned that these guns, augmented by a further four at Hoxa, would be enough to protect Hoxa Sound against torpedo craft. Destroyers carried out a mock attack and were considered to have been satisfactorily repulsed.

The idea behind this exercise was that the Royal Marines could form a 'flying corps' of 3,000 men, trained to seize and hold bases for naval use, and that the defence of Scapa Flow could be assigned to a portion of this body. As ever, the costs of defence were foremost in some minds. In June 1912 the Chief of the War Staff was minuting: 'Assuming that it is necessary to maintain in time of peace a permanent garrison of 250 Marines in order to protect the anchorage from an unexpected *coup de main* the only further economy to be anticipated would be by appropriating 4.7-inch guns already in stock which would reduce the estimated cost from £40,000 to a nominal £10,000 and the substitution of huts such as at Aldershot for solid barracks. It is possible, however, that the stormy weather in the Orkneys may be an argument against this class of accommodation.' In July the Marines stayed in tents, but the assessors of the exercise recognised that any length of stay would require huts capable of 'standing strong winds'. In the Second World War, many of these lessons had to be relearned.

The July 'invasion' of Flotta seems to have been generally regarded as a success. Before the Marines had landed in Kirk Bay, the permission of the Marquis of Zetland, the owner of the island, had been quietly sought. After the exercise, the farmers on Flotta had put in some small claims for damage to grazings and turf, and were compensated by being left the quantities of stakes and barbed wire the Marines had abandoned.

The War Office estimated the cost of fortifying the Flow a little short of £400,000; this was too much, and the sum was revised downward in 1912 to £190,000 for the initial build-up and a further £29,000 for maintenance. This was achieved by having fixed defences for only some of the channels and by using the local TA personnel instead of regular artillery forces. It was recognised that Scapa Flow would be an unpopular posting for the Royal Marines but the planners hoped that, by counting the tours of duty in the islands as sea-time, this particular pill would be satisfactorily sweetened.

The advantages of the Flow as a war anchorage were seen as threefold: it was big enough to hold the entire Grand Fleet; its isolated, insular position gave security against spies observing ship movements; and the hydrographic conditions of the approaches made submarine attack 'practically impossible'. In 1912 the potential of the submarine was unrealised and attack by surface craft armed with torpedoes – German destroyers or small fast cruisers operating from the Norwegian coast – was seen as the 'only danger'. The Flow was to be defended by blocking narrow entrances and guarding the others. A third option, to have the Fleet defend itself, was dismissed as demanding too much from the seamen: the effect of maintaining constant readiness was unknown, and there had to be a place where the ships' crews could relax in security.

The visits to Scapa Flow had made navy captains familiar with northern waters. The Navigation Department of the Admiralty could write in June 1914 that the Flow posed no problems as an anchorage for battle-cruisers, battleships and large fleet auxiliaries and 'no navigational problems in leaving at any state of the tide'.[8] The earlier decision to develop the Cromarty Firth rather than the Flow as a permanent base, with the Flow being held as a war anchorage without fixed defences, was reversed in 1913 when the provision of fixed defences for the Flow was recognised to be 'a matter of urgency'. It was decided that the Admiralty would be solely responsible for the defence of Orkney and Shetland.

Fig. 3 (previous page) *Hammocks stowed in a Ness Battery accommodation hut during the First World War.*

Fig. 4 (above) *Dining al fresco at the Ness Battery during the First World War.*

Fixed gun defences under naval control, now reckoned to cost about £80,000, and a garrison of 250 Marines on HMS *Scylla* as depot ship were proposed. By July 1914, the Admiralty had another need to consider – how to defend a new oil fuel dump, holding 50,000 tons of oil.

With Scapa Flow now strategically important, the military authorities became very sensitive to any suspicion of espionage. There can be little doubt that the Kaiser did have agents keen to know what was happening in this new base but the anxiety about spies could take a ludicrous and comic turn. In 1909, two German balloonists had arrived unexpectedly in Orkney when a south-easterly gale caught their craft after they had lifted off from Munich and drove them a thousand miles across Europe to land in the islands; if this could happen accidentally in peacetime, what would the enemy try in war? On the day before the First World War began, Lieutenant James Marwick of the Orkney Royal Garrison Artillery arrested two men who had been sketching the Hoy cliffs. They turned out to be schoolteachers on holiday – one came from Edinburgh, the other from Southampton – but Marwick had concluded they had had a foreign air about them.[9] Early in August 1914 a German trawler was captured

Fig. 5
Officers of the Ness Battery pose with their motorised transport. The bicycle in the centre is on its stand.

and brought into Scapa; the *Orkney Herald* reported that carrier pigeons had been found aboard her and she may even have had a wireless set.[10]

There are rumours and counter-rumours about the amount of spying that went on in Orkney in both world wars; the theme of espionage at Scapa Flow fuelled the plot of a 1930s thriller movie, *The Spy in Black*. One story that gained wide circulation in the Second World War asserted that the success of the attack on the *Royal Oak* in October 1939 was partly the result of the work of a Nazi agent who lived in Kirkwall under the cover of being a watchmaker; no mention of this character was found in German records after the War.[11] In the summer of 1938 a stranger selling religious literature spent some time on the island of Stroma: Sutherland Manson, the son of the island schoolmaster, remembers him as being 'young, very effusive, blond', given to expressing 'an intense desire to obtain a house overlooking Scapa Flow' but never revealing anything of his place of origin.[12]

During both wars, civilian life in a wide area surrounding Scapa Flow was subject to the Defence of the Realm Act, often referred to as DORA, obliged to comply with military needs and governed by stringent regulations. Trespassing, sketching and photography at defended harbours were forbidden, as was the spreading of reports 'likely to create disaffection or alarm'.[13] The people around

BS-172
Albion

Fig. 6
Men of the Ness Battery, Stromness. Note the strap designed to hold down the hut during strong winds.

the Flow were asked not to mention ship movements in private correspondence. Hoxa and Hoy Sounds had examination vessels to interrogate traffic; only boats ordered to Scapa Flow could approach within five miles of Hoxa Sound and only those bound for Stromness could penetrate Hoy Sound from the west. (The Scrabster-Stromness ferry – the redoubtable *St Ola* – continued her daily crossings.) At night or in thick weather, no entry was permitted. Passage through Cantick Sound was forbidden.[14] Fishing boats had to stay within sight of land and return to port before nightfall.[15] In this atmosphere, rumours sprouted and flourished like weeds in the public imagination. One, reported in the *John o'Groat Journal* on 7 August 1914, held that a fierce engagement had taken place off Orkney in which seven German warships had been captured and two cruisers and a merchantman sunk. The yarn was given substance by the observed northward passage of a hospital ship. 'We publish this rumour with great reserve,' wrote the paper's editor, 'not able to unearth the least grounds for its authenticity.'

The Grand Fleet anchored in Scapa Flow late in July 1914. It was under the command of Admiral Sir George Callaghan, who flew his flag on HMS *Iron Duke* and was due to retire in December. The Admiralty, however, had plans to replace him immediately. Thus it was that Admiral Sir John Jellicoe caught the night train from London to Wick, where he arrived on Saturday 1 August only to fiand that fog prevented the cruiser HMS *Boadicea* – sent to fetch him to Scapa – from sailing until the following day. Despite officially travelling north to be Cunningham's second-in-command, Jellicoe sensed that he was about to be appointed in Cunningham's place and protested in a telegram to the Admiralty that this might cause resentment in the Fleet. A second telegram from Jellicoe, after he reached Scapa on the second, brought the response that he should be ready to take over in forty-eight hours.

Cunningham remained unaware of their Lordships' intentions until he received a message from the Admiralty a day later. Early on the morning of 4 August, the same day war was declared against Germany, Jellicoe opened the sealed orders he had been handed when he had boarded the train and found his suspicions confirmed – he was now the commander-in-chief of the Grand Fleet. The somewhat embarrassed Jellicoe later paid a warm tribute to the way Cunningham, his personal friend, had taken the news. The Fleet was ordered to sea at once and, by half-past eight, after the older admiral had gone ashore, the Fleet was under way.[16] Jellicoe now had under his command twenty dreadnoughts, four battle-cruisers, eight pre-dreadnoughts and forty-two destroyers.[17]

At this time, the Flow was not well protected. Indeed, Jellicoe was to wonder why Germany did not attack it with a daring, lightning move with their more powerful and numerous destroyer fleet,[18] numbering eighty-eight in 1914,[19] and he kept the capital ships as much as possible at sea in the early weeks of the conflict. Shore defences were created by sending ashore some twelve-pounder naval guns and the Orkney TA units established shore-gun batteries. Friction was to arise between the local TA soldiers and the Royal Marine reservists detailed to man the guns which was to have repercussions later, in the Second World War.[20] There was nothing in the Flow at the beginning in the way of booms or sea obstacles to prevent an enemy sneaking in.

Battleships and battle-cruisers were expensive to build and man, but were vulnerable to attack by torpedoes and mines. As symbols of British naval might, the loss of such a ship could come as a stunning blow to national morale. That torpedoes and mines were to be taken seriously was demonstrated very early. The cruiser, HMS *Pathfinder*, was torpedoed by a U-boat off St Abb's Head on 5 September, and *U-9* torpedoed three cruisers, HMS *Aboukir*, *Hogue* and *Cressy*, off the Hook of Holland on 22 September, when nearly 1,500 men were lost. The dreadnought, HMS *Audacious*, fresh from the builder's yard, struck a mine in Irish waters on 27 October; all the crew were rescued, but the Admiralty kept the news under wraps until the end of the war. The first merchant ship to fall to a submarine was the British *Glitra* on 20 October near the Norwegian coast.

As the navy was desperately short of minesweepers, fishing trawlers were commandeered for the dangerous task of patrolling ahead of warships to fiand these steel balls of explosive. Before the techniques were worked out, one trawler was sunk for every two mines cleared. The size of the threat can be judged from the fact that during the four years of hostilities the Germans were to lay some 43,000 mines, and over 200 minesweeping vessels were sunk.[21] In all, almost 3,000 trawlers and drifters were commandeered or built for naval service in the First World War, to work as patrol craft, tenders to the warships, escorts, boom attendants, supply boats and any other purpose for which they were suitable. The fishermen, supplemented by naval officers, were adept at handling their craft in all kinds of weather, and many served with distinction in Scapa Flow.

In August 1914, Germany had twenty U-boats ready for action[22] and by the end of the year, the fleet had increased to thirty-five.[23] They roamed the sea as solo hunters of any prey they met. British submarines – the convention of calling the British vessels submarines and the German vessels U-boats, from *Unterseeboot*, was established early – were to act in the same way, but in the beginning the navy did not look on the submarine as primarily an offensive weapon. Two days after the war began, a raiding party of ten U-boats set off for Orkney waters but turned back after some reversals of fortune (one was lost in a minefield and a second was rammed by the cruiser, HMS *Birmingham*).[24]

Only by keeping his big ships on the move in open water, where their speed thwarted stealthy attack by U-boats, could Jellicoe feel secure. Speaking at a celebration dinner after the war, Rear-Admiral H.W. Grant, who had commanded HMS *Hampshire* early in the conflict, recalled: 'We spent one winter in Scapa Flow and the whole time were under steam. At that time Scapa Flow was not a healthy place to live in, because we were never quite sure whether the Hun would get a submarine in. We had a good many scares and had to raise steam. At that time we had not such appliances as depth charges . . . Then we did not know so much of the Germans as afterwards, our wireless not being so effective, and week after week we were constantly going in and out of Scapa Flow at night'.[25] In the first month of the war, the Fleet spent only one whole day in the Flow and, in September, only six. Before the end of 1914, the *Iron Duke*, Jellicoe's flagship, logged 16,805 miles at sea and took aboard over 14,000 tons of coal.[26]

On 1 September there was an alarm in the Flow when it was thought a U-boat had managed to thread its way into the anchorage. At 6 p.m. the cruiser, *Falmouth*, reported a periscope in sight and opened fire on its suspected position; HMS *Vanguard* and a patrolling destroyer followed suit. The Fleet was immediately put on full alert and ordered to raise steam and weigh anchor. Colliers and storeships were instructed to place themselves alongside those capital ships without torpedo netting to shield them from attack. Then, at six-thirty, HMS *Drake* reported a submarine in sight, and Jellicoe ordered all ships to make for the open sea. The fog was closing in rapidly, darkness was falling and there were no navigation lights or beacons, but by 11 p.m. the exodus from the Flow had been accomplished without accident. Two destroyer flotillas were detailed to search the anchorage, now deserted apart from the repair ship *Cyclops*, lying off Scapa with all the telegram and telephone connections. It was still thought that the submarine might have been hit by one of the four rounds fired by the *Falmouth* but no sign of an enemy vessel was ever found.

There were further false alarms but, finally, on 23 November, a real enemy submarine almost made it into the Flow: *Kapitänleutnant* Heinrich von Hennig conned *U18*, a 450-ton submarine with three torpedo tubes and a speed ranging from nine to fifteen knots, around the east coast of the Orkney mainland on the night of the 22nd–23rd. In the early hours, he surfaced close to the Pentland Skerries to wait for the ebb tide to carry his vessel west towards the Hoxa Sound entrance to the Flow. The Skerries lighthouse suddenly came on, as it did in wartime when the Fleet was sailing. As it happened, Jellicoe had ordered the capital ships to Loch Ewe. (On 7 October a report of a U-boat in Loch Ewe had caused Jellicoe to move the fleet to Lough Swilly, and showed that even the west coast might not be beyond the enemy's reach.)

By 11 a.m., *U18* had crept westward far enough to allow von Hennig to see that only a few small ships remained in the area of Hoxa Sound. Shortly after this, the *U18*'s periscope was spotted and destroyers and trawlers raced to hunt for the intruder. *U18* submerged and lay quietly on the bottom until the enemy had passed over him. When von Hennig thought the immediate danger was past, he ordered a return to periscope depth. At the vital moment, the *U18*'s luck ran out. The submarine was struck by a trawler, the *Dorothy Gray* of Peterhead, just as she neared the surface. According to the official record, the trawler, under Skipper Alex Youngson, had been chasing the *U18* but another version of the story, reported by Iain Sutherland, says that the *Dorothy Gray* was limping slowly after the rest of her flotilla and accidentally banged into the U-boat.[27] In any case von Hennig's vessel was now seriously damaged. The *Dorothy Gray* blew urgent warnings on her siren to attract the attention of the searching destroyers, while *U18* submerged and tried to escape eastward. After striking a rock, surfacing, being rammed again by another trawler (the *Kaphedra*) and diving again, *U18* had almost found the safe open water of the Moray Firth when she ran against the Skerries.

At last, his command crippled beyond recovery, von Hennig had no option but to surface and surrender. He ordered the raising of a white flag, which was first seen by an Orcadian, Robert Wilson, on lookout duty at Brough Ness, South Ronaldsay. The Royal Navy, frantically seeking the U-boat, had lost track of her again. Wilson telephoned to report what he saw. A voice, perhaps tired of false alarms, asked him if he could tell a whale from a submarine, to which the canny lookout replied: 'Well, if it's a whale it's got twenty-five men on its back.'[28] The destroyer *Garry* was despatched to the Skerries to rescue the three officers and twenty-three men surviving from *U18* (one German sailor had drowned).

The defences of Scapa Flow were to become considerably stronger as the war progressed, as a later U-boat attack was to prove. The first boom across Hoxa Sound was ready by the end of December 1914 and two more, in Switha Sound and Hoy Sound, were completed early in the following year. Blockships were sunk in the narrow, eastern channels and in Hoy Sound, and lookout posts and searchlight stations were sited in the island ring. A minefield was laid off Hoy Sound. Naval headquarters moved from the exposed Scapa Bay to Longhope in October 1914. In 1919 it shifted again, this time to Lyness. Hydrophone systems capable of picking up engine noise and linked to explosive loops, armed with the newly invented depth charge, were installed. Eyes in the air augmented those of the surface patrols. Balloons were used for observation and were stationed at Caldale, west of Kirkwall, and Houton. They did not prove to be overly useful, as the windy nature of the Orkney weather often kept them grounded; one was carried away in a gale and never seen again, the observer aboard presumably drowning when his uncontrollable craft came down in the sea. The hydrogen-

Fig. 7
HMS Opal, *one of the two destroyers wrecked in bad weather on South Ronaldsay on 12 January 1918.*

filled balloons were also prone to catch fire if the static electricity in the atmosphere reached a critical level.

The weather played a big part in the life of Scapa Flow. In the summer, during the long hours of daylight, it is as tranquil and idyllic a place as any in the north, but in winter, when the weather closes in with lowering, dark cloud and impenetrable showers of rain, sleet or snow, the sun hardly seems to rise at all. Dark and cold, isolated, blasted by seemingly perpetual gales, it is not an anchorage for faint hearts and demands consummate seamanship. In the Second World War, the weather was to cause far more aircraft casualties than enemy action and the ships of the Grand Fleet also found it to be a formidable enemy. HMS *Boadicea* lost her bridge in heavy seas off Shetland on 14 December 1914; and a little over a week later, on 26 December, HMS *Conqueror* and HMS *Monarch* collided while entering the Flow. The Fleet was returning on that occasion from a sweep in the Heligoland Bight. A severe south-easterly gale was blowing funnel smoke across the field of vision, limited already by the darkness of the morning. The *Monarch* altered course to avoid a patrolling ship and the *Conqueror* ran into her. For a short time it was not clear that the damage hadn't resulted from the action of a lurking enemy and the Fleet cleared the Flow. In the time the ships spent in the turbulent Pentland Firth, no further damage was sustained to capital ships but three destroyers had to be sent for repair.

In the autumn of 1915, heavy seas in the Firth tore the forebridge from the battleship *Albemarle* and shifted the iron roof of the conning tower. Two men were washed overboard and lost. A more tragic accident happened close to the end of the war, on 12 January 1918: the scene was set by a fantastic display of one of the Flow's more spectacular natural phenomena. The Northern Lights, aptly termed the Merry Dancers in northern parlance, filled the sky one night with shifting curtains of coloured light; a man on HMS *Boadicea* who stared in wonder at the sight was warned by an older, more experienced shipmate to look out for rough weather.[29]

Fig. 8
Able Seaman William Sissons, the only survivor from the wrecks of the destroyers Opal *and* Narborough *in January 1918.*

The storm struck two nights later. The *Boadicea* was on patrol to the east of Orkney, plunging in a heavy sea in visibility cut to zero by blizzards. Her escorting destroyers, the *Narborough* and the *Opal*, were having difficulty coping with the storm and turned back. Coming blind into the vicinity of the islands, the two ships missed the jaws of the Firth and hit rocks at the Clett of Crura, south of Hesta Head on South Ronaldsay. They did not know where they were and, as they were breaking up under the pounding of the sea, could give no information over their radios beyond the fact that they were in imminent danger and in need of assistance. Only one man from the two crews of 180 men survived: Able Seaman William Sissons managed to struggle ashore from the *Opal* and survived for thirty-six hours on a cliff ledge before being found.

Sir John Jellicoe had travelled north by train to assume command of the Fleet; during both world wars, this was the method of transport taken by most of the servicemen, and the trains came to be known as Jellicoes or Jellicoe Specials. The journey was long – 700 miles from London and further from the south coast naval ports such as Devonport – and uncomfortable, especially in winter. A through-train left Euston and steamed into Thurso at least twenty-four hours later; if the weather was bad, or if there were delays for any reason, it could take much longer, even up to three days. The troop trains often had no heating and no catering, and sometimes limited toilet facilities: they were crowded with bodies, kitbags and equipment, and filled with tobacco smoke as well as more obnoxious odours. A majority of the ratings and soldiers had never travelled much from their home areas and had little knowledge of their destination. One man recalled the journey as being 'gruelling almost beyond imagination'.[30] When the train reached Thurso, the tired, disoriented men stumbled onto the platforms to be driven two miles to Scrabster to catch a boat across the Pentland Firth, a crossing that reduced many of them to seasick wrecks. Generally, the sailor who came to Scapa aboard his own ship, or the airman who flew north, could count himself lucky.

Although it is understandable that the unpleasant side of the long journey would be remembered, it was not always so bad. The summer trains could leave fond memories and, in bad weather, the troops in transit could depend on local support. 'We would arrive in Thurso,' said Geoffrey Davies, who belonged to Shrewsbury and served in the navy during the Second World War, 'to be told that nothing would be moving in the Flow for at least two days. A gale. Schools and church halls were turned into billets, and entertainments – dances, concerts – and food were laid on. A wonderful time! The storm as predicted blew itself out after the weekend, and then the Pentland Firth was busier than ever.'

At last ashore in Stromness or Scapa or Lyness, the soldiers and airmen had a short road journey to their base, whereas the sailor had to take to the sea again in a drifter to fiand the depot ship (HMS *Imperieuse* in the First World War, and the former Union Castle liner, *Dunluce Castle*, in the Second) for his onward posting to his ship. All of this often took place in the dark, and it could be snowing or raining, or at least windy; not the best conditions in which to negotiate the bulwark of the drifter with a kitbag, gas mask and other gear. A few arrivals appreciated the wild beauty of the Firth and the bare, cliff-edged landscapes of the islands, and the sight of the ships in an array of seapower thrilled them. The whole of the Grand Fleet at anchor, the largest fleet of the Royal Navy ever to assemble in one place, was a scene never to be forgotten.

Both the Grand Fleet and the German High Seas Fleet, at its bases across the North Sea in Wilhelmshaven and Bremerhaven, were strategic weapons. A clash between them was anticipated by the public of both countries but it was a clash that senior naval officers wanted to avoid unless assured of a victory. Jellicoe aimed to bottle up the German dreadnoughts on their own shore. He knew that a hasty, ill-conceived battle between the well-matched opponents could result in disaster; that, as Winston Churchill said, he could lose the war in an afternoon. Vice-Admiral Reinhard Scheer, who became commander of the High Seas Fleet in January 1916, was equally aware of his strategic responsibility. For most of the war, naval battles involved only a few ships – for example, at Coronel off Chile on 1 November 1914, off the Falklands on 8 December 1914, and on the Dogger Bank on 24 January 1915. The fleets engaged in only one large-scale conflict in the mighty testing of firepower known to the Germans as the Battle of the Skagerrak and to the British as the Battle of Jutland.

On 30 May 1916, after receiving word in the early evening from Naval Intelligence HQ, the so-called Room 40, that the German High Seas Fleet had started to come out, Jellicoe made his move. Late in the evening dusk, the battle-cruisers left Rosyth under the command of Vice-Admiral Sir David Beatty and the main body of the Grand Fleet, under Jellicoe, left Scapa Flow and Cromarty. The seaplane carrier HMS *Campania* missed the signal to sail and lost two hours in setting off after the Fleet from Scapa: Jellicoe ordered her to turn back, mistakenly thinking that she would never catch up; although the carrier HMS *Engadine*, sailing with the battle-cruiser squadron from Rosyth, flew one of her four seaplanes, aerial reconnaissance played almost no part in the ensuing clash.

The battle took place on the afternoon and evening of 31 May, and action continued through the night until around 4.00 a.m. when the Royal Navy realised that the Germans had returned to port. Casualties on both sides were high: the Royal Navy lost 6,097 men out of some 60,000, three battle-cruisers, three armoured cruisers and eight destroyers/torpedo boats. On the German side, 2,551 men out of 36,000 were killed; and one pre-dreadnought battleship, one battle-cruiser, four light cruisers and five destroyers/torpedo boats were sunk. The ferocity of the encounter in the dark, cold North Sea is brought home by the fact that the figures for the wounded are only 674 in the Royal Navy and 507 in the High Seas Fleet.[31]

The German authorities were quick in releasing the news of the battle, proclaiming a great victory with ecstatic newspaper reports and celebrations. Jellicoe, on the other hand, maintained radio silence during the return voyage to Scapa Flow, leaving the Admiralty with only the German account of casualties, which listed the heavy British losses but kept silent about their own. At first the Admiralty suppressed the German account but then released it in response to the public demand for information. When Beatty's battle-cruisers reached Rosyth, dock-workers gave them a cool reception. The families of the seamen had had a worrying time during this period: for example, the parents of Midshipman William Keith on HMS *Warspite* had to live with the German news

Fig. 9
Heavy seas breaking over an unknown warship, probably a cruiser.

that their son's ship had been sunk until, on the Saturday morning after the battle, he was able to telegram them to say the *Warspite* had arrived back safely in the Flow after 'a rather lively time'.[32] Men on the Flotta gun battery saw the Fleet creep home in the dawn on 2 June with 'no flags flying, no bands playing' and were filled with sadness, as if they were seeing a defeated force limp home to lick its wounds.[33] Jellicoe's slowness in providing his side of the story put him in danger of becoming a scapegoat. Safely back in the Flow he at last broke radio silence and signalled to Whitehall that his ships would be ready for action on four hours' notice, a clear and reassuring sign that the Royal Navy had not been defeated: indeed, it had won a tremendous strategic victory. Jellicoe remained in command of the Fleet until he became First Sea Lord in November 1917 and was replaced as Commander-in-Chief by Sir David Beatty.

Just a few days after Jutland Scapa Flow was again brought to the public's attention. On the evening of Sunday 4 June, Lord Kitchener left King's Cross by train on a special mission to the Tsar to discuss munitions supplies, and other ways in which Russia could be aided. Kitchener, the Secretary of State for War, was the nation's senior soldier – a national hero, the victor of Omdurman and other imperial conflicts. His heavily moustached face was plastered across the country on recruiting posters.

The trip to fortify the resolve of the Russians was Kitchener's own idea and he approached it impatiently. His special train slid into Thurso early on the Monday morning and he hurried to join the destroyer, HMS *Oak*, for the crossing of the Firth to Scapa Flow where Jellicoe received him aboard the *Iron Duke*. The 10,850-ton cruiser, HMS *Hampshire*, had been chosen by Jellicoe for Kitchener's mission – she was considered safe, could do twenty-one knots, and her captain, Herbert Savill, was experienced.

It was intended that the *Hampshire* should leave Scapa Flow by the eastern route, with an escort of two destroyers for the first 200 miles. The weather was appalling on the afternoon of the fifth when Kitchener said goodbye to Jellicoe and his senior officers. Heavy rain driven by a strong north-easterly gale whipped around the men in their greatcoats as Kitchener climbed down from the *Iron Duke* to the Wick drifter *Mayberry* for the trip to join the *Hampshire*. The barometer was still falling and there was every prospect of the gale growing worse. Kitchener, however, was keen to be off. Partly to gain some shelter from the islands and partly because U-boat activity was normally greater on the east side of Orkney, Jellicoe ordered Savill to abandon his initial intention and leave the Flow by Hoxa Sound and pass to the west of the islands.

At half-past four, the Secretary for War was piped aboard the cruiser. An hour later, she was punching westward past Tor Ness on the south coast of Hoy.

Fig. 10
The crew of X Turret on the Iron Duke. *Warrant Officer S.A. Walling, the ship's schoolmaster, sits fourth from the left in the second row.*

The wind was blasting at fifty knots and the *Hampshire* had to cut her speed to eighteen knots. In the high seas, the escorting destroyers, the *Victor* and the *Unity*, were labouring to keep up. At six o'clock the *Victor* signalled that she could make only fifteen knots; Savill ordered her back to base, but then the *Unity* reported difficulty in going faster than twelve knots. Savill cancelled his order to the *Victor* and dropped the *Hampshire*'s speed to fifteen knots. The *Unity* had to reduce speed again and, with the wind and the seas still rising, Savill ordered both destroyers to turn back and decided to go on alone.

By half-past seven, the *Hampshire* was off the west coast between Marwick Head and the Brough of Birsay, down to thirteen knots but still battering on through the storm. To add to the difficulties, the wind had shifted to north-north-west and the cruiser was riding into its teeth. As she passed the coast, little more than a mile from the cliffs, the Fraser family living at Feaval, Birsay, went out to watch her. Suddenly they saw dark smoke, heard an explosion and saw a tongue of flame shoot up from around the gun turret ahead of the foremast. A big cloud of yellowish smoke whipped away over Marwick Head in the wind, recalled John Fraser, then eleven years old. The Frasers watched the

Fig. 11 (previous page) *This remarkable picture, taken aboard the* Queen Elizabeth *in June 1917, shows HM King George V in the centre, with to his left Prince Albert, later King George V, and then serving in the* Malaya; *to his right Admiral Beatty, in profile as was his preferred pose; and in front, holding the dog, Lord Louis Mountbatten, then serving as a midshipman.*

cruiser lose speed, change course and then sink. It all happened in fifteen minutes: the *Hampshire* went down at eight o'clock.[34]

Corporal James Drever of the Territorial forces and other shore witnesses alerted Jessie Comloquoy, the Birsay sub-postmistress, to send a telegram to the naval commander of the Western Patrol in Stromness and to the Royal Garrison Artillery in Kirkwall stating that a battle-cruiser (in the stormy gloom they did not recognise the *Hampshire* as a cruiser) was in distress. The sub-postmistress transmitted this grim news twice and added an appeal for assistance with survivors.

About 200 men got away on three life-rafts from the sinking ship and drifted south in the tossing sea, eventually coming in to the rocky shore between Marwick and the Bay of Skail. The laden rafts overturned in the surf. Most of the seamen were crushed or drowned, and many died of exposure as they tried to drag themselves to safety. Only twelve out of the 655 men on board the *Hampshire* survived the disaster.

It was later reported that when the explosion occurred Kitchener was in his cabin with seasickness but came on deck.[35] The Secretary for War went down with the ship and his body was never recovered. There is still strong feeling in Orkney over the way the naval authorities acted in the wake of the sinking, with an abiding belief that more could have been done to save the men as they came ashore in the raging water. An offer of assistance by the Stromness RNLI was rebuffed, and official search parties were dilatory in reaching the scene. Rescue vessels, including the *Victor* and the *Unity*, did not arrive until some two hours after the cruiser had gone down. Some locals who went to the shore to help survivors were ordered to keep away by military authorities anxious about security and secret documents washing ashore and falling into the wrong hands.

Jellicoe found himself on the morning of 6 June with the melancholy duty of cabling London to report the devastating news. He mentioned that either a mine or torpedo was the cause. There were many rumours and stories that sabotage was involved but, in the end, it emerged that the *Hampshire* had fallen victim to bad luck and incompetence.

A mine-laying U-boat, the *U75*, one of a new class of long-range vessels, had laid some twenty contact mines in what was to be the *Hampshire*'s track only days before the incident, and it is now generally accepted that the cruiser struck one of these. An internal explosion immediately after contact with the mine, possibly of a magazine – which would explain the appearance of yellow smoke – assured the end. It was later claimed that naval intelligence had some knowledge of the mine-laying but had failed to act on this, and that the weather with the shift of wind to the north-west could have been foreseen.

★

Fig. 12
HMS Hampshire.

After Jutland, neither Jellicoe nor Scheer was willing to risk capital ships in a major trial of firepower. On 19 August 1916, the High Seas Fleet made its last excursion in force into the North Sea to bombard the east-coast English ports. The Grand Fleet was forewarned in ample time by the superior intelligence gathering of the Admiralty and set sail to intercept the enemy. The German fleet was using zeppelins for forward observation and one of these mistakenly reported a British force of destroyers and light cruisers as battleships, causing Scheer to turn away from an engagement. Supporting U-boats torpedoed the cruisers *Nottingham* and *Falmouth*, and the British submarine *E23* crippled the German dreadnought *Westfalen*. It was clear to naval tacticians that the submarine and the torpedo were beginning to render the capital ship redundant.

In recognition of this and of Britain's dependency on supply by sea, Germany launched unrestricted submarine warfare against shipping on three separate occasions, the last such coming into force on 1 February 1917. As the months passed, the tonnage of shipping sunk by U-boats increased alarmingly – from 520,412 tons in February to 860,334 tons in April.[36] It has been estimated that over seventy-one vessels were sunk by submarines and seventeen by mines in the northern seas around Orkney and Shetland between 1914 and 1918.[37] The German commerce raider *Möwe* laid some 250 mines in the general area of the Pentland Firth in the winter of 1915–16. The loss of their ships led Norway, a

Fig. 13 (opposite)
Lord Kitchener transferring from ship to ship in Scapa Flow shortly before the departure of the ill-fated Hampshire.

Fig. 14 (above)
Soldiers of a search party formed after the sinking of the Hampshire.

neutral nation, to complain of lack of escort. The north-east coast of Scotland was considered a particularly risky stretch of sea, and British intelligence was aware that the Germans were monitoring ship departures from Bergen and informing U-boats of their approach. The Admiralty approved the introduction of a convoy system for the Shetland–Norway passage in April, although doubts over its use persisted. Opponents of the idea argued that massing the ships would invite torpedo attack and that there was a shortage of escort vessels. The question of protection for North Sea convoys became wrapped up in the larger question of introducing convoys for British shipping in general. Many Royal Navy officers felt escorting to be a poor substitute for offensive action against the enemy, and independently minded merchant skippers did not like having to keep station in convoys at the speed of the slowest vessel. Finally, in April, after the USA entered the war, the convoy system was introduced. The first trans-

Fig. 15 (previous page) *Lord Kitchener and Captain Dreyer on the* Iron Duke, *taken shortly before his departure. Lord Jellicoe has just emerged from the doorway behind them.*

Fig. 16 (above) *A gun crew on an unnamed Q-ship in Stromness harbour.*

atlantic convoy left Hampton Roads for Britain on 24 May[38] and thereafter the losses to U-boats of merchant vessels declined. The navy had re-learned, after a painful wait, the lessons first driven home more than a century before against Napoleon; the convoy system was implemented at once when the Second World War broke out.

Another method adopted to defeat the U-boats was the Q-ship or U-boat decoy ship. Known at first as special service ships, this idea arose early in the war. An armed merchant ship, the *Victoria*, was the first to be commissioned, in November 1914. By the end of 1915, five – the *Prince Charles*, the *Vala*, the *Duncombe*, the *Penhurst* and the *Glen Isla* – were operating from Scapa Flow. The Q-ship was a merchant vessel with the ability to disguise herself as a helpless tramp ship; she sailed alone and could change her appearance, hoping in this way to fool U-boat skippers to come close to attack. To encourage the U-boat's approach, the volunteer crew of the Q-ship put on a display of panic, rushing about and taking to the boats, while some of their number stayed out of sight to ready the guns.

First blood in this deadly game for the Scapa Q-ships went to the *Prince Charles*. Under the command of Lieutenant W.P. Mark-Wardlow, she was cruising near North Rona on 28 July 1915 when she came upon a Danish ship, the *Louise*, and a U-boat, *U-36*, on the surface near her. The U-boat left the neutral Dane and made for the *Prince Charles*, opening fire as she approached. The British crew maintained the usual subterfuge by appearing to abandon ship and the *U-36* fell into the trap. She was sunk by the two six-pounder and two three-pounder guns of the *Prince Charles*, and the survivors were taken prisoner.

The German Navy soon realised the trick being practised on them and became wary of seemingly harmless merchantmen sailing alone; after 1915 the Q-ships did not have a great deal of success. The idea was resurrected in the Second World War but not for long: in December 1940, Churchill wrote to the First Lord of the Admiralty to express his disappointment over their performance and sought views on alternative uses for them.[39] Before leaving the Q-ships, however, it is right to mention the *Ready*. Originally the *Probus*, she was crewed by Orcadians under an Orcadian captain, William Moodie of Finstown, who had his own score to settle with the U-boats – in July 1915, his schooner, the *Sunbeam*, had been sunk by one off Wick. The *Ready*, a brigantine, is also notable for being the first of a handful of sailing ships to be commissioned by the Admiralty in the First World War. Moodie and his crew, some of whom had sailed with him on the *Sunbeam*, had their revenge when, escorting a convoy out of Falmouth on 23 June 1917, the *Ready* sank a U-boat; the gun crew's second shell hit the U-boat amidships and they pumped in all seventeen rounds into her before she went down. Moodie was awarded the DSO for this action.[40]

When the First World War began, the newly established Royal Naval Air Service (RNAS) had three seaplanes and two land-based aircraft ready at Scapa Flow, serviced from a repair base at the farm of Nether Scapa. Later the base was moved to Houton, where the personnel had to endure primitive living conditions. The Houton base and the neighbouring balloon station became quite populous, with 800 men and a further 200 civilian labourers. For a short time, the expansive, enclosed lochs on the Orkney mainland were tried for seaplane landing but they proved to be too shallow and exposed. With an increasing use of aircraft as the war went on, a vigorous debate emerged over how this new mode of transport might best be used in naval warfare. Their role as patrol craft was obvious – Curtiss and Felixstowe flying boats, for example, patrolled the Fair Isle Channel on anti-submarine duties – but how they might be deployed in a more offensive role, coordinated with ships, required experiment.

In 1912, Lieutenant C.R. Sampson RN had flown a Short S.27 seaplane, then known as a hydro-aeroplane, from the foredeck of HMS *Africa* in Sheerness; on his return he had to land in the sea and be winched aboard. This became the standard practice. An ageing light cruiser, HMS *Hermes*, was converted as a

Fig. 17
Colleagues rush to grab Squadron Commander Dunning's aircraft as he tries to land on HMS Furious, *in the first successful deck landing on a moving ship.*

seaplane carrier in 1912; in August the following year she came to Scapa Flow with two aircraft aboard.

HMS *Furious* was launched in 1916 as a light battle-cruiser and modified in 1917 as an aircraft carrier with five Sopwith Pups and three Short 184 seaplanes. When she came to the Flow in 1917, a landing field for the Sopwith Pups was laid out at Smoogro. The seaplanes came down in the sea to be winched aboard as usual but the naval pilots were wrestling with the question of how they might land a Pup on a ship as well as take off from one! They reckoned that, with the *Furious* steaming into a headwind of twenty-five knots, a deck landing should be possible. On 2 August, Squadron Commander Edwin Dunning took off and put the theory to the test. Although the ship's maximum attainable speed was only twenty-six knots and the wind speed that day reached only twenty-one knots, he succeeded in approaching the deck, holding his engine at just above stalling speed, and touching down so that his colleagues could grab the tail and fuselage to bring him to a safe halt.

Dunning made a second successful landing on 7 August but, later in the same

day, during a third trial, disaster struck. Dunning made three passes, each time revving his engine at the last moment and taking off again. At the fourth try, he seemed to be about to land when a sudden wind gust caught the Sopwith Pup and toppled it to starboard where it fell into the sea. Dunning was apparently knocked out by the blow and drowned before he could be rescued.[41]

Fig. 18
Squadron Commander Dunning's aircraft tips over the side during his final, fatal attempt to land on the deck of HMS Furious.

Furious, which at that time did not have a full flight deck, underwent further modifications to improve her facilities as a carrier but tests showed that her superstructure and funnels caused too much turbulence. After the war she was to be rebuilt as a true aircraft carrier. Experiments were made on other ships whereby a ramp was fixed to a gun turret to provide a launching platform. Later, another cruiser, the *Vindictive*, was changed while under construction to become a carrier but she did not join the fleet until the end of the war. In 1918, another new carrier, the *Argus*, was built – the first with a flush, unobstructed deck. The *Argus* had been laid down in 1914 as the Italian liner *Conte Rosso* but was bought by the Admiralty two years later; she was completed too late to see combat in

Fig. 19 (overleaf)
An improvised launching platform on the roof of the forward gun turret on HMS Emperor of India *in Scapa Flow in 1916.*

Fig. 20
Seamen aboard HMS Iron Duke *feeding seagulls in Scapa Flow in the First World War.*

the First World War but served in the Second before being broken up in 1946. HMS *Hermes* was laid down as the first purpose-built carrier in 1918.

A plan was briefly considered in August 1917 to attack the German fleet in its bases with Sopwith T.1 Cuckoo torpedo planes but this was shelved.[42] The RNAS and the Royal Flying Corps were amalgamated in 1918 to form the Royal Air Force, but the special needs of the Royal Navy in regard to air operations led to the formation of the Fleet Air Arm in 1924.

For most of the war, the capital ships of the Grand Fleet swung around their anchor chains. Life aboard fell into a routine of shipkeeping and in Scapa Flow time could hang heavily among the crews cooped up on the water. Officers devised training exercises and entertainment to break the tedium, and laid out a golf course on Flotta. Trips ashore were limited but highly prized. The seamen had plenty to eat – some culinary adventurers came up with a seagull stew, reputed to taste like fishy chicken – and the rum ration must have been a bright punctuation mark in the day's routine. Then there were the shipboard tradesmen – tailors, barbers, shoemakers – who plied their business for the benefit of their shipmates, and, despite the prohibition on gambling, those who ran flourishing Crown and Anchor schools.

The small ships – the destroyers and patrol craft – were much more active, although this did not guarantee a more comfortable existence. The trawlers and drifters patrolling the booms kept to their stations in all weathers and, when the battle-wagons passed in or out, the trawler crew opened a section of the boom, the gate, to let them through, a job that gave them a wonderful view of the big

Fig. 21
Christmas Day 1916 on the Iron Duke. *Chaplin and some other popular figures seem to have joined Beatty for the occasion.*

ships but left them bobbing like corks in the wash. One dark night the cruiser *Shannon* sliced through the trawler who opened the gate to let her in.[43]

'I had a great deal to do with the trawlers and drifters,' said Rear-Admiral Grant, 'and I remember a dour old Scotsman who was the skipper of one of these boats. These men were a little Republic on their own ships; they did not understand the Navy. The old skipper used to stick in his cabin but used to take me where I wanted to go. However, he was a first-rate fellow and did not care what he did. Weather was nothing to him. It was just the same with the men outside'.[44]

Even on the anchored dreadnoughts, however, danger could never be presumed to be far away. The two battleships, *Warspite* and *Valiant*, collided during an exercise on an August night in 1916 in the Flow, and *Valiant* lost thirty feet of her bow. On 31 December 1915, HMS *Natal*, a 13,500-ton cruiser, unexpectedly caught fire and sank quickly in the Cromarty Firth with a heavy loss of life. Bad powder was blamed for this accident, the third of its kind, and, before the war was over, unstable explosives had taken yet more lives. Late on the evening of Monday 9 July 1917, HMS *Vanguard* was at anchor when she appeared to shiver, rise in the middle and release an eruption of smoke and fire to form a crimson light and a mushroom cloud. Seconds after this apocalyptic vision, the shattering sound of an explosion echoed around the Flow, and debris, including a whole gun turret weighing many tons, fell from the shroud of smoke. For a time no one knew what had happened. The *Vanguard* had shattered so suddenly that no signal had been sent and the fact she was now missing had to be established by a process of elimination. Pools of oil burned luridly on the sea

Fig. 22
Prime Minister Asquith leaves the Iron Duke *on the Admiral's pinnace.*

as boats moved in to search for survivors. The battleship had been anchored close to Flotta and the hot metal falling on the island set fire to the heather and whins; seamen were detailed to take a cutter and land to beat out the fires. On the way the sailors passed through a sea strewn with oil, wreckage and broken bodies. In all, 803 men died in the explosion; there were only three survivors, and one of those soon succumbed to his wounds.

As chance had it, a few of the *Vanguard*'s officers were attending a concert on the theatre ship *Gourko*, anchored beside the *Royal Oak*. One of them was Midshipman R.F. Nichols who, when he was second in command of the same *Royal Oak* twenty-two years later, again escaped death in dramatic circumstances.

On 7 December 1917 ships of the United States Navy arrived in Scapa Flow. Battleship Division 9, led by Rear-Admiral Hugh Rodman flying his flag in the 27,000-ton dreadnought *New York*, steamed in through Hoxa Sound. The Squadron had three other battleships – the *Wyoming*, *Florida* and *Delaware* – and together they formed the 6th Battle Squadron of the Grand Fleet. The *Texas* joined them in February and, in July 1918, the *Arkansas* relieved the *Delaware*.[45] The Americans shared the escort of convoys and other duties but one of their roles was the protection of ships laying the Northern Barrage, a vast minefield stretching from the east coast of Orkney clear across to Norway. The aim was to create a barrier to ensnare and destroy U-boats. Over 70,000 mines were deposited but it is still a matter of debate whether the expense, in money and manpower, was worth the result: exact figures are impossible to determine but fewer than ten U-boats are believed to have sunk or been damaged in the Barrage.[46]

By the end of the war the defences of the Flow were very strong. Cables laid on the seabed across the entrances detected vessels passing over them by induction of an electric current; this loop system was linked to minefields. On the night of 28 October 1918, the hydrophones on Stanger Head picked up engine noise when no friendly vessels were expected and the minefields were activated – it was a U-boat. Lieutenant H.J. Emsmann was trying to pilot his vessel, *UB 116*, through Hoxa Sound in a surprise attack. Emsmann saw searchlights sweeping for him but felt confident enough to continue his submerged approach. At half-past ten, his hull activated the cable current to warn the listeners on the hydrophones. The mines across Hoxa Sound were exploded and, when the reverberation died down, engine noise was no longer heard. At dawn there was oil on the surface and other wreckage was picked up. Divers later found and identified the crushed remains of *UB 116*, with the bodies of Emsmann and his crew of twenty-five inside.

Word of the Armistice on 11 November 1918 roused the service personnel at Scapa to joy. The wireless operators at the seaplane base at Houton quickly passed the welcome news to their colleagues; it reached the ships in the same way and sped through the messdecks, the best bit of scuttlebutt heard for a long time. By the end of the war, Beatty had shifted the centre of Grand Fleet operations to Rosyth but on the ships remaining in the Flow, including such American vessels as the *Arkansas*, the celebrations were wild.

A few hundred miles away, across the North Sea, the High Seas Fleet had troubles to deal with. After Jutland, the German capital ships did not venture to sea in strength. Moored in Wilhelmshaven, Kiel and other ports, the crews grew bored and finally mutinous. Some officers and men volunteered for transfer to submarines or destroyers where there was still the opportunity to see action, leaving morale to wither among the others. On 2 August 1917, men on the dreadnought *Prinzregent Luitpold* refused duty and went ashore in protest. The leaders were imprisoned or shot. In other incidents German seamen were forced to level their guns at their comrades to maintain discipline.[47]

Fig. 23 (overleaf)
HM King George V climbs a ladder to the Queen Elizabeth *after visiting a vessel described on the original photograph as simply a 'picquet'. It resembles a submarine but could be a surface craft of some kind. The destroyer* Castor *met the King in Scrabster. The man standing third from the left looks like Prince Albert, the future King George VI. The censor has scrubbed out some unknown but sensitive object, but has seen fit to leave in the other capital ships anchored in the Flow. This was most probably taken during the King's official visit in June 1917.*

Fig. 24
HMS Vanguard,
photographed in 1912.

For all their problems with discontented seamen, the German Admiralty, under Admiral Hipper, still had an intact fleet. The Armistice presented them with the problem of what to do in view of the peace negotiations now under way. Some felt that a final offensive could not bring about a German victory but would inflict such damage on their opponents' navies that the Fatherland would be able to bargain from strength. It would also be an honourable act, as the meek surrender of great ships, undefeated in battle, was unthinkable.

The low morale and mutinous behaviour in the Fleet, however, meant any plans for assault had to be abandoned. At the end of October 1918, some battleship crews refused to obey orders, and Hipper and his officers had to cow them into submission by setting destroyers to target the ships with torpedoes at close range. The tense showdown ended with the ringleaders being taken off to prison. Discontent continued to simmer below decks and the mutiny spread to shore establishments. Seamen and workers set up revolutionary councils on the Soviet model, and red flags were hoisted in several towns. Any concerted action against the Allies became impossible. Appalled by the action of their colleagues and overcome by shame, some officers sneaked to sea on a U-boat, intending a suicide raid on Scapa Flow, but their vessel was spotted off the Scottish coast and rammed.

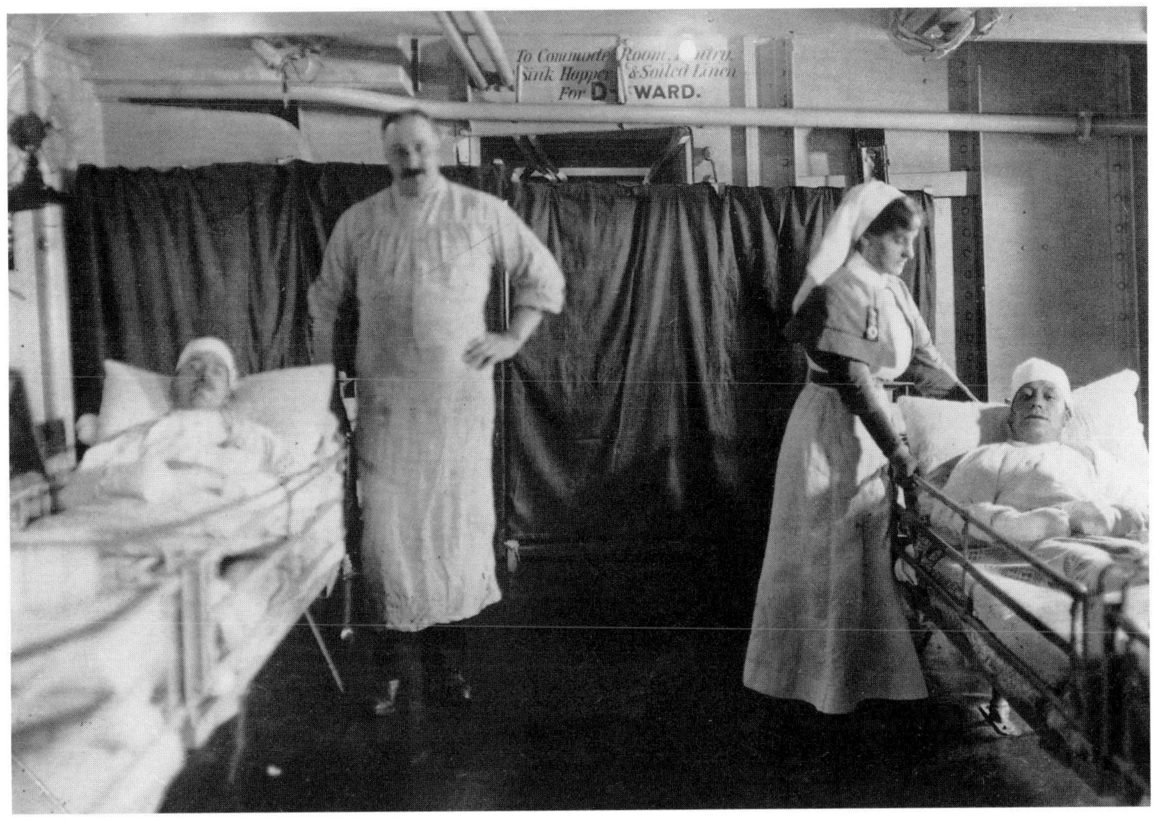

Fig. 25
The two survivors of the Vanguard *disaster.*

In the Armistice terms the immediate fate of the German fleet was laid down in black and white. Article XXI stated that the U-boats were to be handed over to be shared among the victors (most of them were eventually scrapped), and Article XXIII dealt with the seventy-four surface ships by stating they were to be interned in neutral ports or, failing that, Allied ports. After some delay and consideration, the Allied Naval Council decided that Scapa Flow was the only anchorage in which they could be held securely; Beatty was put in charge of the operation to receive them. Article XXXI of the Armistice expressly forbade destruction of the ships – some officers on both sides were already aware of the possibility of scuttling.

The details of the internment conditions were negotiated and, finally, after some hasty preparations, the German fleet steamed out of the North Sea haze on the morning of 21 November to rendezvous fifty miles east of the Isle of May with the Royal Navy ships detailed to escort them into captivity. Britain was jubilant. The German seamen felt humiliated, feelings enhanced by the hostile behaviour of their escort who were desperately ready to counter any treacherous, last-minute acts of defiance. After the ceremonies in the Firth of Forth, the German ships were ordered to sail in groups to Scapa Flow and by 27 November they had all arrived in what effectively was a prison.

★

The surrender and internment of the High Seas Fleet was widely reported in the British press, but sometimes the accuracy of the voices raised in triumph and still keen to denigrate the Hun was far astray. 'Shortly after the arrival of the German fleet,' ran one story, 'parties of seamen attempted to land on one of the islands, but were turned back by a picket boat. Under cover of darkness, however, a raid seems to have been made on a flock of sheep. Boats' crews of Germans also came alongside some of our cruisers, pleading for food. To ensure their strict confinement to their own vessels, all boats were removed from the German ships.'[48] The Germans kept their ships' boats, although there were tight restrictions on their use.

Over the winter of 1918–19 the seventy-four ships lay in their appointed berths in the Flow. The five battle-cruisers were anchored in a line along the Hoy shore, with the eleven battleships to the north-east ringing the islet of Cava. Eight cruisers lay slightly further eastward towards Houton, and the destroyers were tied up in ranks close to Lyness, between Hoy and Fara.

As the months dragged by, some thousands of men were repatriated to Germany, leaving caretaker crews aboard. For them it was a lonely time, bound by imposed regulations; they were not allowed ashore and contact with the islanders and British seamen, except for the crews of tending vessels, was forbidden. This did not prevent it happening and the men on the drifters cheerfully took part in the clandestine trading between the ships. The authorities turned a blind eye, knowing that it would have been impossible to stop fraternisation completely, but the German seamen languished nevertheless in a largely cheerless and depressing tedium. The conditions aboard the ships were made worse by the fact that they had been built with a strategy of foraying in mind and were ill designed to provide long-term accommodation.

The commander of the German fleet, Rear-Admiral Ludwig von Reuter, had a distinguished record in combat and was, by all accounts, a man with a high sense of honour. He fulfilled his distasteful duty as best he could, attending to details of supply of food, tobacco and other necessities, and struggling to maintain morale among the men and some semblance of readiness in the ships. Over the winter he successfully held his 5,000 disconsolate, rebellious followers in some order.

The spring drifted into early summer and, with the lengthening days, came disturbing news from the Versailles conference table where the fate of the fleet was being decided. Fearing the peace terms would bring a 'specially bitter decision', Reuter ordered any celebrations to commemorate the Battle of Jutland on 31 May to be discreet and low-key. Some destroyer crews, generally in finer

Fig. 26 (previous page) *HMS* Queen Elizabeth *passes the stern of the American battleship USS* New York.

Fig. 27 (opposite) *HM King George V and Beatty conversing on the deck of the* Iron Duke *in Scapa Flow. The King made several visits to the base during the war, and King George VI continued this tradition between 1939 and 1945.*

Fig. 28
The ship's company of the Iron Duke *taken on the day of Lord Jellicoe's departure from command of the Grand Fleet in December 1916.*

fettle than their colleagues on the capital ships, ignored this order and strung up lights and bunting, a little to the discomfiture of the drifters keeping an eye on them. Fears among the Germans that the Royal Navy would do something hostile by way of their own celebration were not realised.

A last repatriation draft of 2,700 men left Scapa Flow for Germany on 18 June. By this time the peace negotiations were reaching a climax. Early in May the German government had been presented with terms demanding the handover to the Allies of the interned ships and a reduction of the German navy to a token force. News from the outside world was slow in reaching Reuter and generally he had to rely on four-day-old copies of *The Times* to fiand out what was happening. In the meantime, the Royal Navy had formed plans to seize the German ships to prevent scuttling but they could do nothing to implement them as long as the fleet had interned status.

The deadline for the acceptance of the peace terms by the German government was set for noon on 21 June. Reuter only learned of this on the day before from his four-day-old *Times* and no one took responsibility to inform him officially. The peace terms, as he read them, were devastating: the Royal Navy stood poised to act on the twenty-first but, at a late hour, the deadline for signing the peace terms was extended to 7 p.m. on 23 June. Reuter remained unaware of this.

Fig. 29
The German battle-cruiser Seydlitz *takes up her moorings in the Flow.*

On the morning of the twenty-first, Vice-Admiral Sir Sydney Fremantle, the commander in Scapa Flow, took his battleships to sea for exercises, leaving only two destroyers in Longhope along with the depot ship and the tenders. Reuter, however, had already formed his plan, fearing a pre-emptive seizure by the Royal Navy. On 17 June he had issued orders to all his captains, stating: 'It is my intention to scuttle the ships only if the enemy should attempt to place himself in possession of them without the consent of our Government. Should our Government concur with the surrender of our ships in the peace conditions, then the ships will be given up, to the lasting shame of those who put us in this position.'

Fig. 30
SMS Hindenburg *in Scapa Flow. One of the fleet of drifters who acted as tenders can be seen beyond the bow.*

Word of his intention, which at this stage did not mention a date, was passed to senior officers only but the news leaked on some ships, though without reaching the ears of the guarding force. Ironically the written copies were passed through the German fleet by the unwitting drifter crews in their usual shipkeeping rounds. When he read *The Times* report about the 21 June deadline, Reuter knew the moment had come to act and he issued the

Fig. 31
The German fleet in Scapa Flow.

order to carry out the scuttling on the morning of that day.

The morning of Midsummer Day was warm and sunny in Orkney. A group of schoolchildren from Stromness set off for an outing on the *Flying Kestrel*, a small steamer that had served as a water boat during the war, to view the interned fleet. On the cruiser *Emden*, Reuter issued the final order to begin scuttling at ten-thirty. The coded expression was 'Paragraph eleven: confirm'. It was repeated from ship to ship across the Flow by morse and semaphore, and did not reach the end of the line of destroyers until about an hour later. The drifter crews saw some extra activity and some flags but did not catch on to their significance. As it happened, the *Emden* had two drifters and a watering tender alongside and Reuter could not scuttle his own ship until they drew away at noon.

The first to go down was the battleship *Friedrich der Grosse*; at 12.16, her bell tolling the alarm to abandon ship, she turned over and sank. The *Flying Kestrel*, with the schoolchildren aboard, was as far south as Lyness by this time. Some German sailors had thumbed their noses at the passing children and one of their teachers had explained to them that they should feel sorry for the men held as prisoners so far from home. Suddenly the *Flying Kestrel* received a signal that the

German fleet was sinking and that she should make back for Stromness at once. As she ploughed back north at full speed, the children were presented with the unforgettable sight of a whole battle fleet sinking around them. The noise and the chaos of tilting hulls frightened the younger children but Katie Watt, then aged eighteen, found it fascinating.

After disembarking the children, the *Flying Kestrel* returned to play her part in the efforts of the small British force to stop the scuttling, and took in tow the nearest battleship, the *Baden*, and succeeded in beaching her. The disastrous news was radioed to Fremantle's fleet at sea but, in the two or three hours it took the Royal Navy ships to return, most of the German fleet sank. The destroyers *Vespa* and *Vega* hurried from Longhope. Firing broke out and in the confusion sixteen German sailors were wounded and eight shot dead (a ninth was later shot aboard the *Resolution* by a British sailor). By teatime it was all over. Five battle-cruisers, ten battleships, five cruisers and thirty-two destroyers were on the bottom of the Flow, some still showing parts of their superstructure to mark where they had gone down; and the others had all been beached. The German crews, exhilarated after their winter of captivity, were prisoners under guard.

Fig. 32 *German seamen fishing from the deck of their destroyer.*

Fig. 33 (opposite) *The* Bayern *sinks.*

The British authorities officially condemned Reuter's breach of the Armistice regulations but privately were glad they no longer had to deal with the problem of the fate of the German navy. On 23 June the Admiralty decided to leave the ships where they lay, and on 28 June the peace treaty ending the First World War was signed in Versailles; on 15 September the Royal Navy closed its headquarters in Kirkwall. On 15 February the following year, Scapa Flow reverted to peacetime status.

One vessel from the German fleet – von Reuter's admiral's barge – survived the scuttling to provide useful service as a fast, seagoing ambulance for the people of the Longhope area. Other relics of the internment are on display in Stromness Museum – brass propellers, bells, a binnacle, pieces of machinery, a compass, clocks, cutlery and china, some of it encrusted with barnacles after its sojourn under the waters of the Flow.

Admiralty surveyors had a look at the German fleet a few days after the scuttling and, saying there was no danger to navigation from the abandoned vessels, decided to salve those beached and leave the others where they rested. The sunk ships lay from twelve to twenty fathoms under the surface but the masts and towering superstructure of some of them did prove to be an obstacle. Trawlers cutting through the Flow from the Arctic fishing went aground several

Fig. 34
A salvage party board the scuttled destroyer G102.

times on the hull of the *Moltke*. Something had to be done: meanwhile the local fishermen, carrying on a tradition of the sea, paid clandestine visits and stripped the ships off anything of use they could reach. In 1922 a company called the Stromness Salvage Syndicate bought a destroyer and towed her to Stromness to be broken up. In the hands of the resourceful islanders boiler tubes became curtain rods[49] and, if guns were not beaten into ploughshares, the material found many equally peaceful uses.

In 1923, J.W. Robertson, convenor of Zetland County Council, won a contract from the Admiralty for the salvage of four destroyers. A year later, another contract was made with perhaps the most famous firm to take on salvage in the Flow, Cox and Danks. Robertson's firm used barges with complex lifting apparatus and patented balloons to raise his destroyers. The first one, *S131*, was secured in August 1924 and by the end of the year Robertson had salved his four. Some rivalry developed between the two companies but Cox and Danks had much larger ambitions than Robertson and soon won out in the contest.

Ernest F.G. Cox was a colourful personality, a larger-than-life character with a swashbuckling, can-do air. (Danks had been his partner in the early days of the company but in 1918 Cox had bought him out.) He came from Wolverhampton

Fig. 35
The whaler Ramna *aground on the upturned hull of the* Moltke *two days after the scuttling of the German fleet.*

and learned his considerable engineering skills in a variety of jobs before, with Danks, making shell cases during the war. The firm diverted its focus to shipbreaking in 1921, based at a yard on the Isle of Sheppey. At the centre of his plans for Scapa Flow, Cox had a large floating dock and two ex-Admiralty tugs. He was lucky in finding for his salvage officer a Glaswegian engineer called Thomas McKenzie who had switched in his early career from shipbuilding to salvage and had worked with the Clyde Navigation Trust and, during the war, with the Admiralty. The company set up its headquarters at Lyness, in the former Royal Navy encampment, and at its height employed some 200 men.

In August 1924 they salved their first ship, the destroyer *V70* which, as the price for scrap metal was low at the time, they kept and converted for use as a floating workshop. The acquisition of a larger floating dock speeded up the work and within a year the company was salving destroyers at the rate of about one a month. With practice the rescue of the smaller ships became almost routine – one took only four days to raise. Ten of the destroyers were towed to Rosyth to a breaker's yard, and the others were dealt with at Lyness. Now, Cox was ready to take on the salving of the capital ships.

First, the *Hindenburg*, the biggest battle-cruiser in the fleet. Although her masthead, funnels and fighting top were visible above the surface and the foredeck was just awash at low spring tide, her hull was sitting squarely on the seabed seventy feet down. The floating docks used to prise the destroyers from their graves were no use on such a monster. Cox and McKenzie decided to use the technique of pumping the water from the hull to make it buoyant; success depended on patching the ship to make her as watertight as possible, a job for divers working in the dark to locate holes, ports and valves and seal them. Patches varied from small ones for covering portholes to plates, many feet in size and weighing tons.

The General Strike in the summer of 1926 drove the price of coal beyond what the salvers could afford and brought work to a standstill; Cox needed 200 tons a week, too heavy a cost now for the firm to bear. Typically, he solved the problem by finding a free supply in the bunkers of another sunken battle-cruiser, the *Seydlitz*. The engineers and divers solved many other technical problems as they met them in the course of the dangerous job they had set themselves. Nature provided a few more – conger eels lurked to bite the unwary, shoals of saith ate the tallow used in patching, whales played around the ships and threatened the divers with the wash from their flukes. Diving at depths greater than ten fathoms (sixty feet) required the men to be very fit. Three died. On another occasion a labourer was killed when a crane jib fell on him. Throughout the years of salvage, however, the work force developed a tremendous *esprit de corps*.

Her hull patched, the first attempt to raise the *Hindenburg* began in August 1926. The pumps, powered by engines on pontoons floating alongside, began to draw the water from her. This was a slow job, interrupted by the need to replace patches and deal with other difficulties. At last the battle-cruiser was afloat, but a strong north-westerly gale on 2 September defeated the men's efforts. Patches sprang, the pumps could not keep up, and the *Hindenburg* sank again.

Leaving her where she lay, Cox turned to the *Moltke*, lying between the islands of Rysa Little and Cava, upside down and listing. The plan this time was to pump compressed air into the ship through steel tubes, designed as airlocks, fitted to openings cut in the hull. It took nine months' work to free the *Moltke* from the seabed but, at last, in June 1927 she was up and could be towed. In May 1928, the great ship undertook what was to be her last voyage, the crew living in huts installed on the upturned hull, towed by three ocean-going tugs, ironically enough chartered from a Hamburg company (Hitler was later to forbid German firms from taking part in the salvage).

In the Pentland Firth, the tugs were unable to maintain way against the tide and heavy seas. The *Moltke*, as if unwilling to leave Orkney, dragged the little flotilla west. Waves washed over the hull and flooded the crew's huts and the shelters for the compressors whose job it was to keep up the air pressure inside the battle-cruiser. Then the tide turned, the weather eased and the ship and her escort were able to struggle eastward until they were safely past Duncansby

Head and en route for the Firth of Forth. Here more adventures awaited – they nearly snagged on Inchgarvie Island and almost ran against the Forth railway bridge – but eventually the German ship was safely inside the drydock at Rosyth.

Cox and McKenzie renewed their assault on the *Hindenburg* in January 1930 and this time they were successful – by the end of July she was up, the largest ship ever salved to that date. Another ship was raised twice, this time deliberately. By now the efforts of the salvers had become famous and, in 1928, when the *Seydlitz* was ready to be raised, Cox arranged for the press and the movie news teams to be on hand. Unfortunately, through an error of judgement in pumping air inside her, the battle-cruiser popped up too soon, while Cox was on holiday in Switzerland. He ordered her to be sunk again so she could be raised on cue.

In all, Cox and Danks raised thirty-three of the German ships, including two battleships and four battle-cruisers. The last one, the *Prinzregent Luitpold*, was salved in the summer of 1931 and towed to Rosyth in the following year. Shortly after this, the company, Metal Industries Ltd, and its managing director, Robert McCrone, who had been buying and breaking up the raised ships, took over the task of raising them as well. Cox retired but Thomas McKenzie stayed on to work for the new employer. McCrone had a better head for business than Cox and, through more advanced techniques, including the use of liquid oxygen, and better administration, realised an average profit of £50,000 on the ships they salved – Cox had ended his career out of pocket.

Throughout the 1930s, Metal Industries Ltd raised five more battleships – from the *Bayern* in 1934 to the *Grosser Kurfürst* in 1938 – and were at work on the battle-cruiser, *Derfflinger*, when the Second World War began. The *Derfflinger* was afloat by that time but, as no resources could be spared to tow her away, she spent the war moored in the Flow upside down with a small gang of men to look after her. Thomas McKenzie was appointed chief salvage officer to the Admiralty and, after serving as principal salvage officer for Allied operations in northern Europe, retired in 1945 with the rank of Commodore RNVR.

In all, during the 1920s and 1930s, thirty-eight ships had been freed from their sojourn on the bed of Scapa Flow to yield 327,000 tons of steel. Now, the remainder were left until the return of peace.

The Second World War began on 3 September 1939 but, on this, the second time around for it to become a major naval base, Scapa Flow was better although still not adequately prepared. As the political situation in Europe grew more and more perilous throughout the 1930s, some steps had been taken to strengthen its resources and defences to make it the main base of the Home Fleet. The

Fig. 36
A German ship being towed upside down to the breaker's yard in the Firth of Forth. The men lived in the huts on the hull. The tall cylindrical structure is an airlock through which air could be pumped to keep the hull afloat.

commander-in-chief, Admiral Sir Charles Forbes, knew the Flow well, as he had been a staff officer for Jellicoe on the *Iron Duke*, had fought at Jutland and, by 1918, had captained the cruiser *Galatea*.

However it was touch and go. The improvements to the Flow were not implemented until the spring of 1938, although some decisions had been taken the year before.[50] In June, the laying of anti-submarine booms began and the first, between Hoxa Head and Quoyness, was in place by September. Two other booms, between Innan Kneb and Hackness and between Houton Head and Scad Head, were finished in the spring of 1939. Work began in February 1939 on the Hatston airfield, which became operational in August. Observation posts were set up and manned continuously by the coastguards, who logged all movement of aircraft and shipping.

Commander O.M. Frewin was appointed in February 1939 as the Senior Naval Officer and King's Harbourmaster. He set up his headquarters initially in the Kirkwall Hotel but, in the early days, many of his duties were bedevilled by a lack of funds. For example, he had no boat – a peculiar difficulty to face a harbourmaster – and in June he had to borrow a speedboat from the RAF to call on a visiting French naval squadron. He asked for a new quay to be erected at Lyness to keep the oil fuelling jetty clear of small craft and colliers but, as it was costed at £38,000, it was not built. In July he at last had a teleprinter connection to Rosyth. By then the accommodation available at Lyness was judged to be enough for eighty-five people, which must have been viewed cynically in the light of an expected influx of 1,200 in the event of war.

The *Iron Duke*, Jellicoe's flagship at Jutland and one of the last four coal-burning battleships built for the navy, appeared in August in a new role – stripped of two turrets, she anchored off Lyness as a floating administration block for Admiral Sir Wilfrid French, the ACOS (Admiral Commanding Orkney and Shetland). Commander Lewin moved his headquarters to Lyness. A 12,000-ton steamer, the *Voltaire*, was despatched to Lyness to serve as an accommodation ship but she proved too large to moor close to shore and was transferred south again after a couple of months.

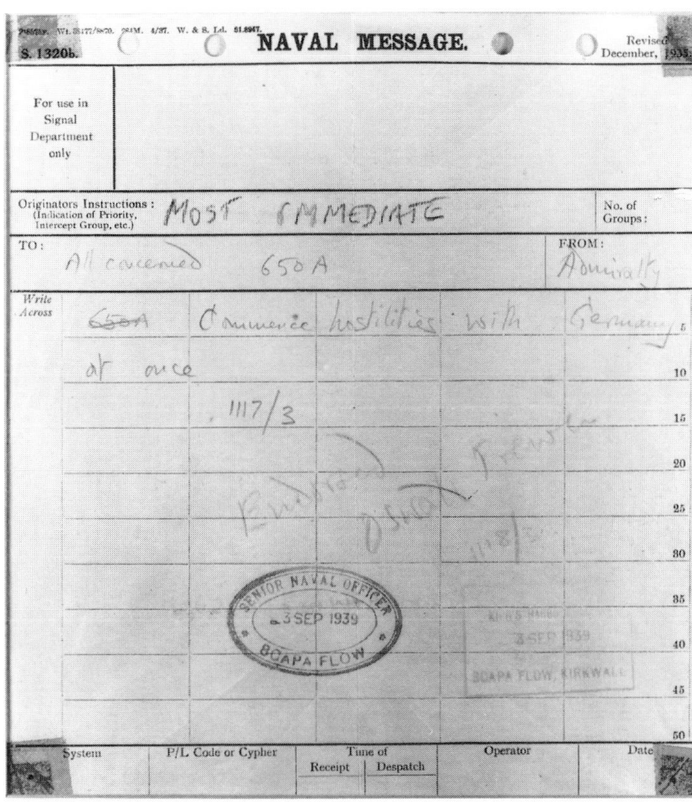

S. 1320b. NAVAL MESSAGE. Revised December, 1935.

For use in Signal Department only

Originators Instructions: (Indication of Priority, Intercept Group, etc.) MOST IMMEDIATE

No. of Groups:

TO: All concerned 650A

FROM: Admiralty

Write Across

650A Commence hostilities with Germany at once

1117/3

SENIOR NAVAL OFFICER 3 SEP 1939 SCAPA FLOW

SCAPA FLOW, KIRKWALL

System | P/L Code or Cypher | Time of Receipt | Despatch | Operator | Date

Fig. 37
The signal announcing the outbreak of the Second World War. It is endorsed by Oswald Frewin, the King's Harbourmaster.

Fig. 38 (overleaf)
A naval aircrew at Hatston.

At the end of August there were forty-four ships in the Flow, including the carrier, HMS *Ark Royal*, with a squadron of Skuas, and the battle squadron comprising the *Nelson*, *Rodney*, *Resolution*, *Royal Sovereign*, *Ramilles* and *Royal Oak* with their attendant cruisers and destroyers. Forbes took the Fleet to sea on 1 September, leaving only a few ships in the anchorage, to begin the strategic duties of guarding the route from the North Sea to the Atlantic, supporting the Northern Patrol between Shetland and Iceland, protecting convoys and enforcing the German blockade. The flagship, HMS *Nelson*, had earlier arranged for the deposition of Admiral Nelson's uniform, carried like a holy relic, in a bank vault in Thurso for the duration.[51]

The civilian contractors, Balfour Beatty and Baldry, Yerburgh and Hutchinson, were hired to build tunnels and install oil storage tanks at the main re-fuelling point at Lyness. Sixteen tanks, capable of holding 100,000 tons of

fuel, were built above ground and were ready by July 1939. The sixth and last of the underground tanks was not completed until August 1943. Many of the civilian workers were recruited locally but others came from far afield; two Irish workers were killed when the roof of a tunnel fell in. The labour force lived in huts. In January 1939, forty-two workmen from the English Midlands walked off the job in protest against bad pay and conditions and, for a few days, after they had crossed the Firth to Thurso, presented the authorities with the problem of what to do with them – they were sent home.[52]

Much still needed to be done at Lyness after the war started. Antony Bridges, a London barrister ruled out of active service in the navy by a disability, volunteered his cutter *Mermaid* for carrying cargoes of gelignite from Scrabster to Baldry's construction site. He noticed on his arrival that the only pier at Lyness was a partly rotten, small, wooden structure; this haven served until, in 1941, a drifter rammed it and knocked it to pieces.[53]

The land defence forces had not been neglected. During the 1914–18 conflict, coastal defence had been the responsibility of Territorial (TA) units recruited in Orkney or transferred from other parts of the country. They had operated under Royal Marine officers, a point of some contention that was to cause further dispute in 1939.

In May 1938, the Orkney TA began to recruit men for a gunnery unit. Within a day they were almost up to strength and the remainder came forward in the following two weeks. The unit was called the 226th Heavy Anti-Aircraft Battery RA, TA; and half were initially posted to Caithness, the others remaining in Orkney. Two further units were formed later in 1938: the Orkney Heavy Regiment RA, TA to man coastal guns, and the Orkney (Fortress) Company RE (T) to operate searchlights.

The War Office plans for the land defences specified eighty heavy and forty light anti-aircraft guns, 108 searchlights and forty barrage balloons. Churchill reduced these numbers to save on manpower. The navy preferred to have its land bases defended by Royal Marines and, now in 1939, the Admiralty found fault with the way the Army was doing things – they were too slow in preparing the batteries and costing too much – and considered deploying Marines again. With unhappy memories of service under Marine officers, these proposals were not popular among the islands' soldiers. Supported by his Director of Local Defence, Vice-Admiral T.H. Binney, the ACOS, wrote to tell Churchill this in December 1939 and finally – though not until June 1940 – it was decided to leave the coastal and anti-aircraft defence of Scapa Flow in the hands of the army. By this time, the defenders had had their baptism of fire.

In September 1939, there was a considerable artillery force in place around the Flow. 226 Battery had eight 4.5-inch anti-aircraft guns at Lyness; and the

Heavy Regiment manned two six-inch guns and one 4.7-inch gun at Stanger Head, Flotta, and two more six-inch guns at Ness, just on the outskirts of Stromness. Men of the 39th LAA Battery from Linlithgow defended the radar station at Netherbutton, in the parish of Holm, with three Bofors guns; companies of Royal Engineers and the 5th Battalion of the Seaforths, with the

Fig. 39
Lyness base under construction.

Fig. 40
The army camp at Ness.

addition of men from the 7th Gordons in October, guarded the gun emplacements.

OSDef (Orkney and Shetland Defence Force) was commanded by Brigadier Geoffrey Kemp MC, RA, a man Hetty Munro, who worked on his staff, was to describe in her diary in 1941 as 'rather gangling and reddy haired – walks badly. His uniform never fits. Rather a delightful smile and, I think, rather shy and scared of the ATS'.[54] For all her criticism, Munro liked Kemp and, with her colleagues, was moved when, in the spring of 1940, he thanked his staff for making the Flow safe for the navy. It had been a considerable achievement. In October 1939, he had arrived in the islands with only a sergeant/clerk, a driver, one car and one typewriter with which to staff and equip his headquarters in Mackay's Hotel, Stromness.

Fig. 41
Men of the Territorials at a lookout post on Rousay.

Formidable though they sound, the defence arrangements were in the early days still compromised by a shortage of guns and equipment, muddled communications, inadequate radar and port facilities struggling to cope with the traffic. Attempts to solve the problems and develop a detailed, comprehensive plan for

Fig. 42
Some of the ten lorries shipped from a firm in Tooting, London, to Lyness for use in constructing roads. The workmen came from Thurso. The foreman, John West, is wearing the hat and has his hands in his pockets.

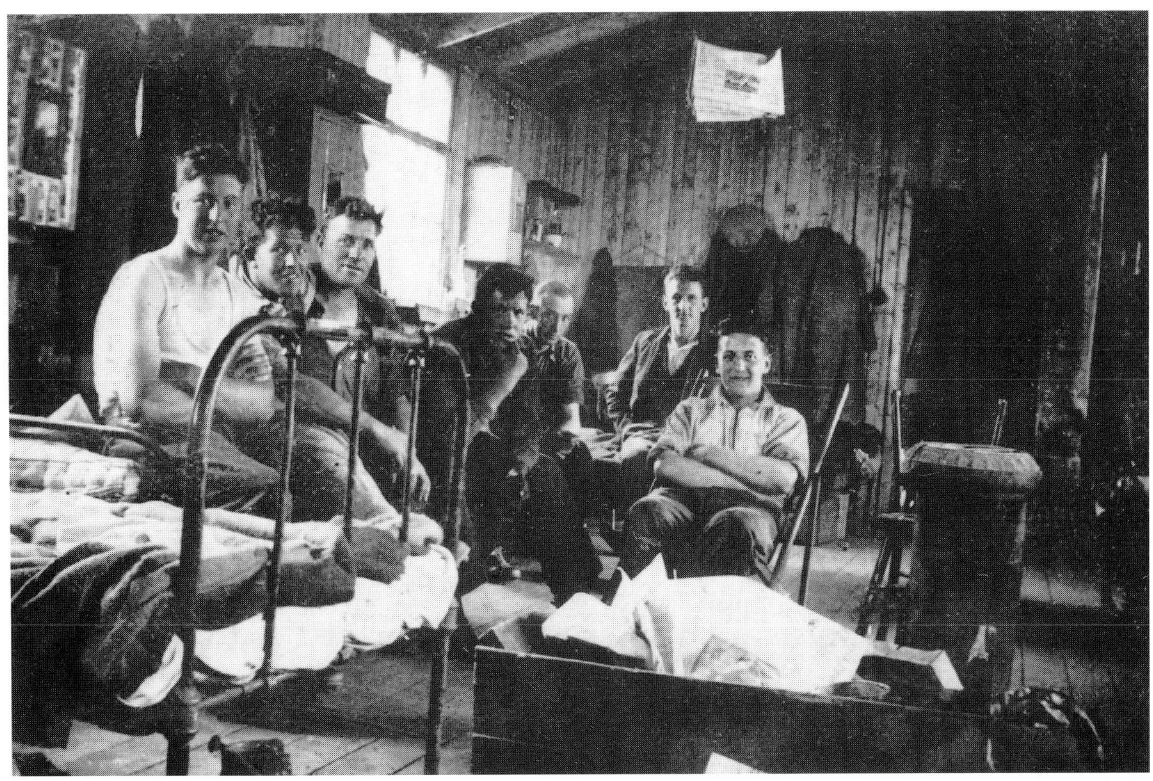

Fig. 43
Civilian workmen in their hut at Lyness.

Fig. 44 (overleaf)
The North Pier at Lyness, with drifters.

the defence of the Flow were to continue for some years and the final 'R' plan, as it was called, dealing with all aspects of defence, did not emerge in fact until 1943.

The threats to the Flow were seen as attacks by U-boat and from the air. Torpedo assault was expected from Day One[55] and on 14 September *U-39* attacked HMS *Ark Royal* off St Kilda. (*U-39* was captured after being disabled by depth charge.) It was well known for U-boats to try to avoid detection and sneak through guarded entrances by 'hiding' under surface ships. Hospital ships, whose special status ensured they always sailed alone and kept lights on at sea, were a favourite vessel for this kind of subterfuge. There were alarms, as Roddy Macdonald witnessed from HMS *Valiant* in March 1940 and recorded in his Midshipman's Journal: 'In the last dog [watch], just before passing through the boom in Hoxa Sound, the screening destroyer reported a submarine in sight to starboard. However, this was a false alarm and we passed into Scapa Flow astern of HMS *Hood* who appeared to get into difficulties in entering the gate'.[56] As a further foil against U-boat attack, dummy warships were anchored in the Flow, created by building false superstructures on the hulls of commandeered liners.

The entrances to the Flow were guarded more or less as they had been in the First World War. In addition to the anti-submarine booms, indicator and guard loops lay on the seabed across the Hoxa Sound approaches to warn of any vessel

Fig. 45
The King's Harbourmaster, Scapa Flow, Commander Oswald Frewin RN (centre, behind lifebelt) with his staff.

crossing their activated field. In tests carried out before the war, a boom had stopped the 28,000-ton battleship, *Resolution*, at seven knots. Anti-submarine nets, made from interlinked loops of steel, hung in the water like giant chain-mail shirts. A section of net, 900 feet long, weighed forty tons but could be laid in place in four minutes.[57] The Hoy Sound entrance was also equipped with indicator, guard and mine loops and a boom across the Bring Deeps. The Flow's Achilles Heel, however, lay on the east side, where the channels between the chain of islands connecting South Ronaldsay to the mainland were strewn with sunk blockships to render them impassable, inadequately as it soon turned out.

HMS *Scott* surveyed the eastern channels before the war to fiand where the blockships should be placed. The first of these, the *Madja*, arrived in Water Sound in February 1939 and there were eventually to be twenty, the last one, the *Inverlane*, being sunk in place as late as May 1944. In keeping with the tradition of penny pinching, the Treasury placed a limit of £10,000 on the cost of a blockship and the purchase of at least one had to be foregone because the price demanded was too high.

On 14 September, Winston Churchill, at this time First Lord of the Admiralty, left London by train for Wick and on the fifteenth crossed to the

Flow. He inspected the anchorage and entrances with the booms and nets, and was assured they were as good as in the last war with improvements being implemented or planned. Churchill stayed on HMS *Nelson* with Admiral Forbes and on 17 September sailed to visit the rest of the Fleet in Loch Ewe, at the time seen by the Admiralty as an anchorage safer from the attention of long-range bombers than Scapa, although its defences were also poor. The First Lord had last visited here in September 1914 to see Jellicoe's fleet. The problems were still much the same but Churchill also found 'the perfect discipline, style, and bearing, the ceremonial routine . . . unchanged'. The ships were old and this seemed to produce in him misgivings – 'a strange experience, like suddenly resuming a previous incarnation' – but he drew reassurance from the fact that the Empire was still intact and Britain still had command of the sea. When he returned to London, he was greeted with the news of the loss of HMS *Courageous*, sunk in the Western Approaches by *U-29*. It was not long before grim news came from Scapa Flow itself.[58]

The German naval command was well aware in 1939 of the weakness of the defences on the east side of Scapa Flow. Commodore Karl Dönitz, in charge of the U-boat fleet, knew that one of his submarines had the ability to thread its way among the blockships and effect entry to the anchorage, and selected *U-47* under *Kapitänleutnant* Gunther Prien for the task. Hence, on 13 October, Prien and his crew lay submerged off the east coast of Orkney waiting their chance. Shortly after seven o'clock in the evening, *U-47* surfaced and set course for Holm Sound, the gap between the mainland and Burray. A passing merchant ship forced Prien to submerge for a short time but by half-past eleven he was on the surface again and conning his ship towards the islands. In his log, Prien recorded that it was a very clear night and, although the land was dark, the Northern Lights were shedding an eerie glow in the sky and the blockships lay like ghosts in the wings of a theatre.[59]

Two to three days before, the steam drifter *Lunar Bow* had found navigable gaps between the blockships. The *Lunar Bow* was one of a flotilla of five drifters on patrol duties; she was commanded by a sub-lieutenant and had a midshipman as navigator and a cadet as first lieutenant, and these keen young officers and the ratings aboard were all 'on release' from the cruiser *Belfast* to which the drifter was attached as a tender. The cadet was later to become Vice-Admiral Sir Roderick Macdonald KBE and in one account of the exploit he wrote: 'on patrol at high water in a flat calm, and after a great deal of discussion and much sounding with hand lead, *Lunar Bow* gingerly transitted Kirk Sound outwards, and then returned to the Flow by Skerry Sound on the other side of Lamb Holm'.[60]

The drifter officers knew that a surfaced U-boat had a similar draft to their

vessel, and signalled the finding of proven gaps in the defences to their superiors. It later emerged that a civilian tug had already passed through the same space but the men on the *Lunar Bow* did not know this. A blockship was, in fact, on her way north to plug one of the gaps. The *Lunar Bow*'s evidence was not presented at the subsequent official enquiry into succeeding events, and it seems that her signal had been ignored. Possibly the senior staff had too much on their minds and they knew more blockships were on their way. Two days after her exploit in Kirk Sound, the *Lunar Bow* was withdrawn from patrol and despatched westward to follow the Fleet to Loch Ewe. As fate would have it, this opened the way for the approach of *U-47*.

Fig. 46 (opposite)
An anti-aircraft gun battery overlooking the outskirts of Stromness and, beyond, Hoy Sound, the western entrance to Scapa.

Fig. 47 (above)
A six-inch gun of the Ness Battery.

Prien took his U-boat through Kirk Sound, passing between the islet of Lamb Holm and the village of St Mary's on the mainland. The tidal current threatened to throw him off course but cautiously he slid past the blockships, scraping over their mooring cables, by alternate use of his port and starboard engines. Just as the U-boat was coming through this obstacle course, car headlights fell upon her: the German seamen immediately felt they had been discovered – they could see sentries and trucks on the nearby shore – but the car swept on, the lights left them in shadow once again and, although Prien did not know this, no alarm was raised. By half-past midnight, *U-47* was through and loose inside the Flow.

In the clear night, Prien at first saw no large ships. In case of just such an attack, Admiral Forbes had taken most of his fleet away west to Loch Ewe. Prien finally spotted under the bulk of the mainland hills two 'battleships' and some

Fig. 48
Wooden decoy ships at anchor in the Flow.

Fig. 49 (below)
The anti-submarine boom stretches across Hoxa Sound from Hoxa, on the north-west corner of South Ronaldsay, to Flotta.

Fig. 50 (opposite)
Towing the floats for a boom from the quay at Lyness.

destroyers. The two capital ships were in fact the seaplane transport, *Pegasus*, and the battleship *Royal Oak*, which had remained in the Flow with the intention of following the rest of the Fleet on the fourteenth. The U-boat fired three torpedoes. One was seen to hit the more northerly of the two targets, the *Royal Oak*, the other two missed. Unsure of the effect of his attack, Prien set loose the torpedo from his stern tube while the bow tubes reloaded, but this weapon missed the *Pegasus*, at which it had been aimed. Then the U-boat fired three more torpedoes and, in this salvo, two hit the *Royal Oak*.

As alarm broke out, Prien ordered full speed and made his escape back out through Kirk Sound, once more skilfully navigating through the blockships. By two o'clock *U-47* was in the open sea and heading for home.

Fig. 51
The boom defence boats Barranca *and* Barcastle.

The impact of the first torpedo to hit the *Royal Oak* caused puzzlement rather than alarm. The explosion took place in the vicinity of a paint store but, apart from fumes and smoke close to the spot, nothing seemed to be amiss. Many of the crew went back to sleep. The noise, however, roused the men aboard the drifter, *Daisy II*, moored on the battleship's port quarter. Skipper John Gatt from Aberdeen didn't know what it could have been but, his senses alerted that something might be wrong, he pulled on his seaboots and hailed the Officer of the Watch on the *Royal Oak*, while his own crew slid back into their bunks. The Officer and Gatt discussed what might have happened and then the drifter skipper noticed straw and wooden staves floating around the stern of the ship. Familiar with this as the packing material normally wrapped around stores and knowing that it was stowed towards the ship's bows, Gatt and the Officer concluded there must have been some kind of internal explosion that had blown the packing into the sea. Just at that moment, twelve minutes after the first explosion, Prien's second salvo of two torpedoes hit the *Royal Oak*.

These fatal blows blasted a gaping hole in the starboard engine room, sending smoke and spray towering over the superstructure – the stricken ship listed quickly as the sea poured in below decks. As the bulge of the hull rose the *Daisy II* was lifted and was in imminent danger of turning turtle. Some men had already slid down the mooring lines from the ship's deck above. Gatt ordered his cook to cut the mooring lines with a knife but before this could be done the strain tore the mooring bitts from the drifter's deck. The *Daisy II* slid down the *Royal Oak*'s side with a thump, but at least she was clear and upright. Lighting acetylene lamps in the wheelhouse, Gatt began his rescue work.

Below decks on the *Royal Oak*, the lights went out, a magazine caught fire, fumes from burning cordite spread through the venting system and the tannoy system failed. The crew struggled in the darkness to find their way to the upper

Fig. 52
Wrens wrestle with the steel rings of an anti-submarine net at Lyness.

Fig. 53 (overleaf)
Churchill talks to some destroyer captains on HMS Tyne, *the depot ship, in Gutter Sound.*

deck, where many slid or jumped into the cold sea, but most of them were trapped in the sudden disaster. The *Royal Oak* sank only eight minutes after she was hit for the second time.

Surgeon-Lieutenant Dick Caldwell was in his bunk when the first torpedo struck. The explosion, muffled and distant, made him get up and dress, and, out in the quarterdeck flat, he found some other officers discussing what it might have been. The second explosion rocked the ship and put out the lights. Wearing a monkey jacket over his pyjamas and one slipper, Caldwell escaped to the deck. As the *Royal Oak* listed and began to sink he was thrown into the sea; avoiding the stern and the propellers, he was tumbled over in the wash before he regained the surface, now smeared in thick oil. Finally, after going down several times and almost giving up, he found his way to an upturned boat where he and about a dozen other men hung on to the keel before being picked up and taken to the *Pegasus*.[61]

After the first explosion, a stoker, Herbert Johnston – his native village St

Mary's was only a short distance away – collected his gas mask and, uneasy about the situation, went to check on the refrigerating machinery that was his responsibility. The second explosion followed by the stink of cordite alerted him to go on deck. Here he saw some of his shipmates getting into the picket boat and followed them. More men joined them. After the ship sank, the picket boat became so overcrowded she capsized. Johnston swam for a time until he was pulled aboard the *Daisy II.*[62] Pay sub-lieutenant Gilbert Harrison escaped by crawling across the tilting quarterdeck and jumping into the sea. Fully clothed, he kept afloat in the water thick with oil by swimming and hanging on to debris until he was picked up.[63] The captain, W.G. Benn, and his first lieutenant, none other than the R.F. Nichols who as a midshipman had escaped the death of the *Vanguard* in 1917, were among the men rescued.

Fig. 54 (previous page) *Winston Churchill, Lord Beaverbrook (third from left) and other senior military and diplomatic personnel photographed at Scapa Flow.*

Fig. 55 (opposite) *The bridge and main mast of HMS* Royal Oak.

Most of the men who survived the sinking owed their lives to the presence of the *Daisy II.* At first there was an orderly evacuation to the drifter but soon the situation turned to every man for himself. The drifter picked up 386 men, many from the sea, and it is said that after she had disembarked the survivors, the oil stains from their presence reached up her funnel, as the huddled men had moved up the superstructure to make room for more of their comrades. The *Daisy II* measured only some ninety feet long with a beam on deck of seventeen feet. John Gatt was awarded the Distinguished Service Cross.

The news of the catastrophe unfolding in the Flow soon reached Kirkwall, two miles away. In the St Ola Hotel, Ella Stephen rose to answer the telephone when it rang at about one o'clock with a request for the resident Royal Navy doctor. When the doctor put the phone down, he asked Ella to bring him a bottle of brandy: 'I'm sure we'll need it,' he said, 'there's been a bad accident at Scapa.' Ella sensed at once that something had happened to the *Royal Oak*; she knew some of the officers, whom she used to drive to the Scapa pier, and she went anxiously to enquire about them but was told nothing at the time. As it happened, most of them survived.[64]

On the Friday before the sinking Sub-Lieutenant Harrison had been ashore in the town with his wife, who was in Kirkwall on holiday. Mrs Harrison went to Scapa pier on the Saturday but was puzzled to see no sign of her husband's ship. She did not learn what had happened until she heard the news in a Kirkwall shop, and thereafter must have spent an anxious time until her husband managed to send a telephone message that he was safe.

The Orcadians donated clothing for the survivors and Ella Stephen recalled how a sailor on the train south from Thurso was to wear a pair of plus fours given by her uncle. The survivors were billeted in houses in the Caithness town, where children sought them out for autographs and a dance was organised for them in the Town Hall on 18 October.[65] The blockship *Lake Neuchâtel*, destined

Fig. 56
HMS Royal Oak *turns at speed in Scapa Flow.*

for the gap through which Prien had eased his U-boat, arrived in Orkney, one week too late, on 21 October.

When the *U-47* reached Wilhelmshaven on 17 October, the crew were fêted as heroes and flown to Kiel and on to Berlin to be received by Hitler himself; Prien was decorated with the Knight's Cross of the Iron Cross. The *U-47* was nicknamed 'the bull of Scapa Flow' and a cartoon of a charging bull was painted on the conning tower. In his statement to the House of Commons on 20 October, Churchill acknowledged that Prien's exploit had been a remarkable demonstration of 'professional skill and daring'. A year and a half later, in March 1941, *U-47* was one of a pack of six U-boats that attacked an Atlantic convoy; nothing was heard from her after the action, in which two other U-boats were sunk, and it was presumed that Prien and his men had been killed in action.

About a year after the sinking of the *Royal Oak*, the hospital ship *Vasna* was moored close to the wreck site and Geoffrey Davies, serving as a sick-berth attendant, recalled that in certain conditions of light and tide the hazy shape of the hull could be made out under the water. For Davies it was a poignant sight, as he had walked under the battleship when she had been in drydock in Devonport before the war.

Fig. 57
The Lunar Bow *among the blockships (line drawing by Roddy Macdonald).*

The most immediate consequence of the loss of the *Royal Oak* was the Home Fleet's reluctance to use the Flow as an anchorage for any length of time until the defences could be made secure. Churchill announced in the House of Commons that Scapa Flow was no longer a base, which was not strictly true but may have diverted German attention. It was, in fact, some six months before the Fleet returned in force to make the Flow a permanent home.

The Admiralty was soon to implement a scheme to prevent any craft ever again creeping into the Flow through the eastern channels, but the threat of airborne attack remained. During the first months of the war the northern coast found itself in the front line, as the Luftwaffe targeted Scapa Flow. To strengthen the defences and to provide operational bases for offensive operations over the northern seas, four airfields were established in Orkney. Until 1937 the Fleet Air Arm had remained under RAF control, a situation unsatisfactory to the Admiralty and one that had held up the development of naval aviation. The standard naval aircraft at the time were the Swordfish biplane torpedo-bomber, the Skua fighter-dive bomber and the Roc and Sea Gladiator fighters which, although they were to perform daring exploits, were outdated.

Work began in February 1939 on the Hatston field, just to the west of Kirkwall; it was operational by August and was commissioned as HMS *Sparrowhawk*, the first purpose-built RN air station in the UK. The construction of Skeabrae, a second station, began in December 1939; in May 1940 it was handed over to the RAF but remained the base for Fleet Air Arm squadrons until RAF replacements could be spared from the Battle of Britain. Grimsetter, an RAF station, was not completed until the autumn of 1940. It was later transferred to the Fleet Air Arm as HMS *Robin*, and later still transferred back again to the RAF. Today it is Kirkwall Airport. Finally, the Fleet Air Arm station at

Fig. 58
U-47 *about to berth.*

Twatt was commissioned as HMS *Tern* in April 1941. Five dummy airfields were also laid out but they proved to be no distraction to German bomber crews and were finally abandoned.

Fig. 59
Above a scribbled cartoon of perhaps Neville Chamberlain, Gunther Prien stands on the conning tower of U-47 *at Wilhelmshaven.*

At the start of the war, RAF Fighter Command established its Sector Station HQ in Wick, in the primary school on the northern edge of the town near the airfield. Control of fighter operations over Orkney was transferred in October 1940 to RAF HQ in Kirkwall and Wick became a base for Coastal Command, but, until then, six squadrons of Hurricane and Spitfire fighters flew from Wick as part of the air defence for Scapa Flow. Castletown airfield became operational as another Hurricane and Spitfire base in June 1940, and an airfield at Skitten a few miles west of Wick was added in December 1940. Dounreay airfield, still under construction when the war ended, was named HMS *Tern II* and in July 1944 began to be home to Fleet Air Arm forces.

Over the period of the war, Orkney was the base at various times for nineteen RAF squadrons and seventy-two Fleet Air Arm squadrons, although many were transient visitors, flying in and out from aircraft carriers, and only three squadrons, engaged mainly in such non-combat duties as training and reconnaissance, were resident throughout the war. For all that, the airfields in Orkney often found their facilities stretched.

A radar station, the first of a series, began operating at Sumburgh Head in Shetland in December 1939. Known as Admiralty Experimental Station I (AES I), it was supplemented in the succeeding months by two on Fair Isle, and single stations on Unst, South Ronaldsay and Dunnet Head, the latter three not coming into operation until the autumn of 1940, too late to play a role in defence against the severe air attacks. An earlier radar post, the most northerly of a chain of twenty stretching the length of the country to Portsmouth, was set up at Netherbutton, in the mainland parish of Holm, before the outbreak of the war but it had primitive equipment and an antiquated procedure for raising the alarm, no more than a telephone connection to ACOS.

In the winter of 1940, an RAF barrage balloon squadron joined the Scapa Flow defences, and some balloons were flown from trawlers in the Flow itself. A base for the balloon trawlers was set up at St Mary's. In a 90 mph gale one balloon on Cava 'uprooted its winch' and dragged it for 600 yards across the moor and over the cliff into the sea.

With effect from 1 December 1939, Orkney and Shetland were made a Protected Area. This meant that 'no persons other than existing residents, Servicemen or police will be allowed to remain in or enter the area without permit'.[66] Permits could be obtained from offices in London or Edinburgh and an application, accompanied by two passport photos and the applicant's identity card, had to be signed by a Justice of the Peace. A so-called Green Identity Card was then issued but this was not enough to gain entry to the Protected Area and had to be supplemented by an additional permit, usually issued three weeks after the

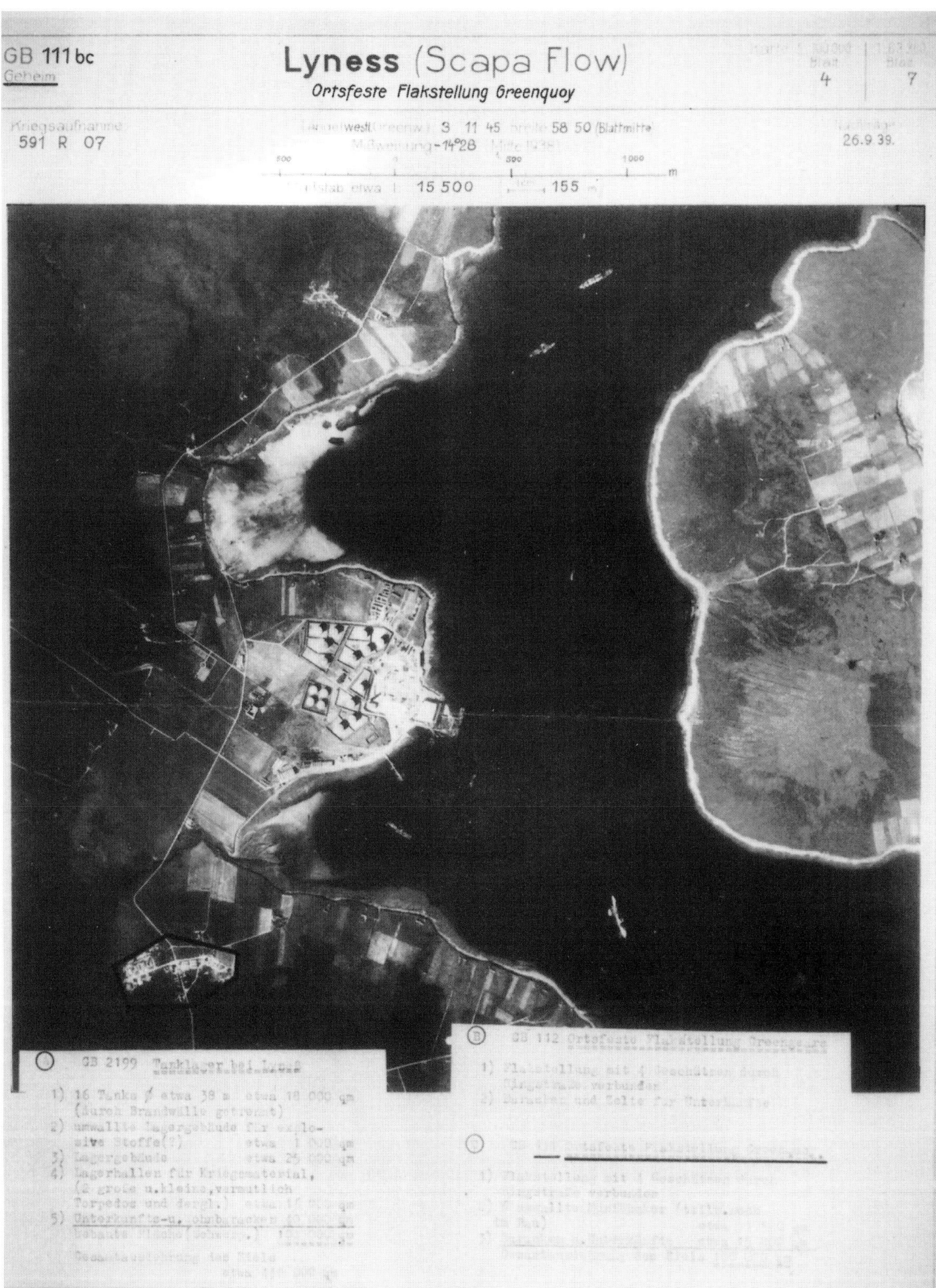

GB 111 bc
Geheim
Lyness (Scapa Flow)
Ortsfeste Flakstellung Greenquoy
4
7
591 R 07
3 11 45
58 50 (Blattmitte)
-14°28
26.9.39.
500
0
500
1000
m
15 500
155
GB 2199
1) 16 Tanks ∅ etwa 38 m
4) Lagerhallen für Kriegsmaterial,
(2 große u.kleine,vermutlich
Torpedos und dergl.)
B
GB 112 Ortsfeste Flakstellung

Green Card and after Scotland Yard had had time to check the applicant's background. Civilian baggage was searched at Scrabster and, in Orkney, a visitor was subject to constant surveillance. Service personnel were exempt from these procedures, their paybook judged to be sufficient as a passport. In the newspapers Scapa Flow was never to be named and was referred to customarily as 'the Northern Base'.

Fig. 60 (opposite) *Luftwaffe aerial picture of Lyness taken on 26 September 1939.*

Almost from the outbreak of the war, the Luftwaffe flew high-level reconnaissance aircraft to try and ascertain the status of the defences and the deployment of the Fleet. The first air raid took place on 17 October 1939. In the first wave of the attack, four Junkers 88 bombers, from Hornum on the island of Sylt on the north-west German coast, came over shortly after ten o'clock in the morning; two dived from high altitude and managed to hit and damage the *Iron Duke*. One of this pair became the first German aircraft to be shot down by a ground-based gun when it was hit by a shell from a battery at Lyness manned by the 226th. It crashed by the Pegal Burn on Hoy; the wireless operator survived by baling out and was taken, injured, to the hospital ship in the Flow. Three hours after this attack, a second wave of fifteen Junkers 88s struck, this time causing no severe damage and suffering the loss of one of their number to anti-aircraft fire: the bomber crashed into the sea between Hoy and Stroma.[67] A Belgian trawler in the Pentland Firth found a German bomb falling uncomfortably close; and a fishing boat from Stroma turned for home when the fishermen felt they were in the danger zone.

The *Iron Duke* was holed by the bombing and she tilted violently twenty-five degrees to port as the sea flooded into a boiler room and spread through her innards. All the lights went out and her complement began to abandon her. Then the listing stopped and a tug, the *St Martin*, towed her into the shallows to beach her safely in Ore Bay. Sir Roderick Macdonald records a story that, he admits, 'may even be true'. As all hands on the *Iron Duke* mustered on the quarterdeck before abandoning ship, they took off their boots. After the successful beaching, the officers and men retrieved their footwear, with the exception of the Admiral who unluckily could fiand only an outsize pair of Royal Marine boots where his own had been.

The destroyer, HMS *Eskimo*, came alongside the *Iron Duke* to provide power for lights and pumps but had to withdraw again during the second raid later in the day. The doughty battleship settled as the sea continued to seep into her. The expertise of the salvage crews from Metal Industries Ltd came to her rescue: in the weeks after the raid, they patched the hull and pumped out the water. (These skilled salvage experts did much valuable work throughout the war.) On 11 December the battleship was towed to Longhope and re-beached.

Fig. 61
The Royal Navy manning anti-aircraft guns at Yesnaby.

She survived more air attacks and carried on, still leaking but at a rate that the pumps could handle. Moored fore and aft, she stayed firmly aground except for her stern which was prone to float at high water and, according to Admiralty sources, list impressively during spring tides. She remained in service as a depot ship for small craft, with Admiral Jellicoe's uniform, cocked hat, sword and Bible still in their glass case aft, a silver statuette of her namesake, the Duke of Wellington, firmly on the wardroom table, and shells for the big guns still, reputedly, in her magazine.

The ACOS moved his headquarters ashore after the first bombing. The only place available at the time was a small accounts office where all the staff officers had to fit themselves into a very cramped space – private and secret interviews had famously to be held in the WC, and the Captain's secretary bedded down on a table. Most of the men slept in the canteen. After a short time, however, houses were requisitioned: the ACOS moved into Rysa Lodge; other senior naval and civil personnel took up residence in Orgill Lodge; and other ranks made do happily with the Longhope Hotel. By now the King's Harbourmaster, the patient Commander Frewin, had acquired a launch, a vessel commissioned as HMS *Proserpine*.

★

Fig. 62 (above)
Anti-aircraft guns line the sea's edge in Scapa Bay.

Fig. 63
Like a collapsing cartoon elephant, a barrage balloon being manhandled on the island of Fara. (With permission from the Ken Kelly Collection, 3 Ardsley Terrace, Irvington on Hudson, NY 10533)

Fig. 64
The anti-aircraft barrage above Scapa Flow. HMS Berwick *is in the foreground.*

Fig. 65 (below)
Plotting in the Fighter Direction Station at Twatt.

Fig. 66 (opposite, top)
A group of soldiers at Hatston beside what appears to be the entrance to an air-raid shelter.

Fig. 67 (opposite, below)
A drifter in Gutter Sound.

During the first raid, many people turned out to watch the dramatic action in the sky above the Flow. 'The weather was very fine on that October day,' wrote Norman Glass in Wick, 'and it was an awe-inspiring spectacle as, amid thunderous droning of planes, the guns of ships and shore batteries rattled up hundreds of rounds and produced curtains of bursts in the sunny and almost cloudless sky'. 'Schoolchildren were particularly difficult to chase indoors,' noted

the *John o'Groat Journal*.[68] Observing the bright trails of tracer and the shellbursts during raids was to become common, dangerous though it was, and long after the war bits of aircraft, shell cases and pieces of shrapnel were kept in homes on both sides of the Firth as souvenirs. George Manson, the schoolteacher on the island of Stroma in the middle of the Pentland Firth, wrote to the local authority in Wick to say they had seen the approach of the bombers in the first raid and asked for an improved telegraph service for early warning. He was unaware of the potential of radar, feeble though the Scapa Flow capability was in the beginning.

There were no raids on during the dark months of 1939–40. The weather was bad that winter, with gales and snow blizzards, and, after the death of the *Royal Oak*, the Fleet spent most of its time elsewhere. During the bitter cold of February and March, a Marine Naval Base Defence Organisation installed emplacements and heavy guns

Fig. 68 (previous pages) *A Swordfish Mk III torpedo bomber converted to anti-submarine duties and equipped with SDV radar.*

Fig. 69 (previous pages) *Scrabster jetty with security control huts.*

to beef up the defences. With the coming of spring, the Luftwaffe turned its eyes on the base once more. Two aircraft had appeared over the islands on 12 February; the air raid warning had been sounded and the schools dismissed, but no bombs were dropped.[69] On 8 March, Flying Officer Dutton, piloting a Hurricane of 111 Squadron from Wick, shot down a Junkers 88 forty miles east of the islands, but this was simply a foretaste of what was to come. At dusk on 16 March, a group of bombers, mostly Heinkel 111s, flew in low and bombed Hatston. In this raid James Isbister, a twenty-seven-year-old employee of Orkney County Council, came to the door of his home at Bridge of Waithe to watch the action and entered history as Britain's first civilian fatality in an air attack, when a fleeing bomber dropped high explosive close by. Two of his neighbours were injured in the same blast; and elsewhere other civilians were wounded, and farm buildings and houses damaged or set on fire. The German news agency later claimed that three battleships and one cruiser had been hit but, in actuality, only HMS *Norfolk* had taken a bomb on her fo'c'sle and three men were killed.

Aboard his small boat tied up at Lyness, Antony Bridges witnessed this raid (in his book he erroneously gives the date as the fifteenth) and wrote: 'Just at dusk . . . something seemed to hit the ship like a blow from a very large hammer . . . the ship was still afloat . . . we tumbled out into the cockpit . . . streams of tracer filled the sky from a score of points on the surrounding islands. The beams of searchlights sprang out and switched to and fro across the dark. More noise of engines rose with the crack of gunfire. Something spun close over us that sounded like a cat whose tail had been trodden on . . . Far away over Flotta, an aircraft, tiny and white as a toy, slid down the beam of a searchlight until it met the outline of the hill, where its disappearance was succeeded by a dull glow.'

A week before, on 8 March, Churchill had been on HMS *Rodney*, accompanying the Home Fleet on its way to re-occupy the Flow when, off the Sutherland coast, a signal warned Admiral Forbes that German aircraft had dropped mines in the vicinity of Hoxa Sound. The capital ships turned to delay their arrival, to give minesweepers time to deal with the threat, and Churchill transferred to a destroyer for the rest of the passage, entering the Flow through Switha Sound.

Churchill was pleased to fiand the defences much improved and strengthened since his last visit – 'not . . . yet complete but . . . already formidable'.[70] Towards the end of March, in a speech to counter the claims of the Nazi propaganda machine, the Prime Minister, Neville Chamberlain, dismissed the latest raid as a failure – it had been unimportant, only to be expected, and only twenty bombs had been dropped.[71] The air raids had, however, revealed the flaws in the air defence. In October the Skuas of 803 Squadron of the Fleet Air Arm had been too slow to engage the enemy; on 16 March the radar station on Netherbutton

Fig. 70
HMS Iron Duke.

failed to spot the incoming German aircraft (Shetland radar had picked them up). To increase the effectiveness of the anti-aircraft fire, the Scapa barrage was created: this new concept, devised by Brigadier Kemp, replaced the earlier, ineffective tactic by which each gun tried to lay on individual aircraft. The Barrage meant all the anti-aircraft guns on shore and afloat co-ordinating their fire to throw up a complete umbrella of exploding shells above the Flow, forcing attacking bombers to fly high. By June 1940, eighty heavy anti-aircraft guns – of 4.5- and 4.7-inch calibre – lay in a ring in an eight-mile radius around the Flow.

The RAF launched a reprisal raid on the Luftwaffe airfield at Hornum on the day after the Scapa Flow raid. The next heavy air attack on the Flow took place on the fine evening of 2 April. The Barrage worked, and the attempts of the bombers to penetrate the murderous curtains of fire failed to achieve any results, beyond two civilian casualties and one wounded serviceman. A Junkers 88 was shot down. One of the retreating bombers, probably in a fit of frustration, fired a machine-gun burst at a trawler in the Firth and strafed Duncansby Head lighthouse. According to Antony Bridges, one barrage balloon sent up during this raid was hit by lightning and exploded in flames, while another, pushed in the strong wind, dragged its helpless winch-lorry into the sea. William Mowatt on South Ronaldsay, who had newly left school, remembers the raids and the answering Barrage vividly: 'wild – Hell let loose'. At Lyness, when the guns fired, the earth trembled and shrapnel fell sizzling in the sea.[72]

A further attack, on the evening of 8 April, lasted for over two hours and was reported in the *John o'Groat Journal*, the Caithness newspaper, as 'another thrilling sensation for the people of this locality, who had a clear view of the German raiders and the reception they met'.[73] This time, radar gave advance warning and the twenty-four bombers were intercepted by Hurricanes of 43 Squadron from Wick. Four of the attackers were shot down by anti-aircraft fire and three more fell to Hurricane attack. One of the Heinkels downed by 43 Squadron chose to land at Wick airfield, where the two survivors of the crew of four were imprisoned.

The heaviest raid on Scapa Flow followed two days later, on 10 April. Sixty bombers – Junkers 88s and Heinkel 111s – were spotted on radar coming in from the east at 18,000 feet. Gladiators of 804 Squadron and Hurricanes of 605 Squadron took off from Hatston and Wick respectively to intercept. About one-third of the bombers evaded the fighter attack and pressed on through the flak of the Barrage to try to hit targets in the Flow, including the protecting booms. HMS *Suffolk*, a cruiser, was hit and some of the crew were killed. Two bombers were shot down by fighters and three fell victim to the anti-aircraft barrage.

Scapa Flow experienced its last air raid of the war – a relatively short, sharp engagement, 'half-hearted' in the words of W.S. Hewison who witnessed it – on 24 April. Twenty-three bombers appeared on the radar plot but only five made a bombing run into the Flow, this time from the west in bad weather with poor visibility. The bombs caused no damage. A solitary Junkers 88 bombed an RAF camp on the island of Sanday on 8 March 1941. There were other small-scale attacks but, apart from high-flying reconnaissance aircraft and these occasional intruders, the Luftwaffe tended to stay away from the northern anchorage. With the invasion of the Low Countries and France, followed by the Battle of Britain, the main theatre of the war in Europe shifted southward.

Intelligence reports of increased movement of enemy shipping in the northern North Sea reached Forbes early in April. On the seventh he ordered the Fleet to sail from the Flow and Rosyth to the Norwegian coast to be ready to intercept any move by the German Navy to break out into the Atlantic. Hitler's target on this occasion was, of course, Norway herself and five towns were attacked in the first phase of the campaign – Oslo, Kristiansand, Egersund, Bergen and Narvik. After two months of fighting, the German assault achieved success and Norway became occupied territory, an outcome with grave strategic consequences for the Royal Navy's control of northern waters.

Earlier on the day of the heaviest air raid on Scapa – 10 April – the Fleet Air Arm struck back at the enemy. Before dawn broke over Kirkwall Bay, sixteen Skuas of 800 and 803 Squadrons took off from Hatston and flew north-east to Bergen, at the limit of their range, to attack the cruiser *Königsberg*. The German warship went down under the air assault, the first major warship to be sunk by aircraft. One Skua was shot down and a second ran out of fuel just as it reached the end of the runway on its return – the raid was otherwise a complete success.

Three more air attacks on enemy installations in Norway took place in the following months. Skuas bombed oil depots and coastal shipping near Bergen in May and again in October, and, also in May, Swordfish from 821 and 823 Squadrons attacked the *Scharnhorst* off the Norwegian coast, although this time the torpedoes failed to find their target and one aircraft was shot down.

As the spring wore on to summer in 1940 and the German army occupied France, the whole country held its breath for invasion. 'The threat of invasion has been brought very close these last few weeks,' wrote Hetty Munro in her diary on 22 June, 'and everyone is on the *qui vive* for something or other. Leave has been stopped and all the wives sent out of the island – this happened about three weeks ago but it is now rumoured they are to get back again. I suppose the idea is that our part of Britain is as dangerous as another nowadays.' In August, she added: 'Orkney has become a complete fortress – how impregnable is not for me to say but I think the Hun would get quite a hot reception if he comes.'

After this time, flights from the airfields around Scapa Flow were limited mainly to reconnaissance patrols and training exercises. This routine defensive work was, however, punctuated on occasion by a brief burst of action. On Christmas Day 1940, a Grumman Martlet from Skeabrae attacked a lone Junkers 88 over the mainland; the German aircraft made a forced landing in a field near Sandwick. Gregor Lamb notes that this was the first kill made by a British pilot flying an American-built aircraft. Another Junkers was shot down into the sea to the east of Westray on 4 March 1941 by three Hurricanes from 253 Squadron at Skeabrae.

Routine flying brought its own dangers. Hardly a month went by without an accident, a state of affairs made worse by the occasional appearance of a genuine enemy. 'Yesterday,' wrote Hetty Munro on 24 October 1940, 'a Hun came swooping out of the clouds about 3,000 yards away from H.8 [an anti-aircraft battery] where practice shooting was going on and played around quite low. The Battery opened fire but of course shot very wide of the plane [towing the target]. Unfortunately they got excited and kept on shooting and the poor old RAC [Reconnaissance Air Craft] who was towing was almost shot up'. Cases of mistaken identity and resulting 'friendly fire' happened whenever returning

Fig. 71
The Heinkel 111 at Wick airport on 8 April 1940, lying crippled after being shot down by a Hurricane from 43 Squadron.

British aircraft lost their way and approached home by an unexpected route. And there was, of course, the weather. After fruitlessly hunting a U-boat off Cape Wrath on 1 April 1940 an Albacore flew into a snowstorm on the way home and crash-landed at Whiten Head. In June 1942 a pilot flying an Albacore lost his way in low cloud and hit the rock stack, Old Man of Hoy. Near the end of the war, in April 1945, a Sikorsky R-4 at Twatt airfield earned the dubious honour of being the first helicopter to crash in Britain.

The Second World War, like the First, brought to Scapa Flow thousands of servicemen and, as in the 1914–1918 period, the majority of them travelled north by rail, reviving the nickname 'Jellicoe' for the often overcrowded, badly heated, slow trains lumbering north through darkened towns. Deep snow in the winter of 1940–41 brought about possibly the longest journey on the route, when one train that left London on 3 February did not steam into Thurso until the eighth, the 150 miles from Inverness having taken four days to accomplish. After that occurrence the trains carried emergency rations. An indicator of the increased traffic is provided by the number of tickets issued in the station at Thurso, the end of the line – the total rose from 8,231 in 1938 to 87,207 in 1940.[74] Thurso also had to cope with feeding the masses of troops in transit. Initially the Royal and Pentland Hotels were pressed into service but the demand was too much for them and a NAAFI, operating in the Town Hall, was set up to feed 240 ratings per sitting. Throughout the period of the war it was estimated that 542,000 meals were dished up. The *St Ola* carried over 900,000

Fig. 72
An air-sea rescue launch at speed in Kirkwall Bay.

passengers to and fro across the Firth between 1939 and 1945[75] and other vessels of the North of Scotland, Orkney and Shetland Shipping Company, the 'north boats', *St Ninian* and *Earl of Zetland*, also served as troop transports for the navy and the army respectively. The *Marialta* was also a ferry for naval personnel.

The old liner *Dunluce Castle* was saved from the scrapyard, hastily refitted and moved to Lyness in March 1940 to serve as a depot ship for personnel in transit. She also acted as a floating office block, a ferry terminus, a base for the anti-submarine trawler patrol, and the Fleet post office. During the air raid on 16 March 1940, a fire broke out aboard her but she was beached and re-floated once the flames were extinguished. One of her less happy roles was to receive and take care of survivors. On one occasion, at ten-thirty in the evening, 150 men, filthy with oil, shocked and hungry, arrived aboard her from a ship torpedoed off Cape Wrath; the staff had them cleaned, treated, fed and away by eleven-thirty the next morning.

The Second War at Scapa Flow differed from the First in bringing north a large complement of army and air force personnel, and women – WRNS, ATS (later the Women's Royal Army Corps – WRAC) and WAAF, as well as members of the NAAFI and some nursing and volunteer services, and a few servicemen's wives. One Wren is reported to have been delighted with the Orkney posting because there were rumoured to be 600 men for every woman.[76] As to the feelings of the men, the reader can guess, but, for the record, one officer in HMS *Pleiades*, the headquarters of the drifter pool, noted, a trifle coyly and pompously: 'It would be opening up one's defences to say that the tone or efficiency of the office improved but the language moderated slightly, perhaps, and even though an occasional bill or coo was heard the work went on just the same.'

There may have been exciting prospects for the single man or woman in the ranks but to a few, appointed officially or otherwise guardians of moral welfare, it presented a challenging problem. The women were naturally in great demand. HMS *Tyne*, the destroyer depot ship, ran tea-dances. Wrens were first stationed at Lyness in May 1943 and, when an invitation to a party arrived in their barracks, a poster invited all willing to respond to sign up; the Regulating Officer counted the number departing for the party on the special transport, usually a lorry, and counted them back in when they came home. 'If you had a date the poor man had to collect you from the regulating office and sign for you and also had to see you were back in time . . . If you went out unaccompanied or just Wrens together you were only allowed to walk on a short stretch of the road,' recalled Jeanne Frith.[77]

Between the short bursts of action, during an air raid, an exercise or an offensive operation, there stretched for both sexes long periods of boredom and routine. Especially during the early months of the war the facilities for entertainment were limited – to young people from the cities of the south they must have appeared non-existent. Troops often found they had to make do and mend as best they could. A group of soldiers spent their first night in two unfinished huts on South Walls – and one blew away, leaving the men staring in amazement at the sky. Churchill himself was moved to comment on the meagreness of the amenities to keep up the morale of the troops and asked for something to be done.

Antony Bridges described Lyness in the first snowy winter: 'a few huts strung along the shore, some corrugated iron sheds behind a stone quay, some oil tanks on the hillside; and a dilapidated wooden pier, with two or three drifters tied up in a tier at the end of it. Apart from these, the great sweeps of water and whitened moor lay still and empty in the gloom'.

On Flotta a large canteen offered beer to sailors on liberty – a ticket got you three pints, no more, in an effort to maintain a level of sobriety – and was the only place of entertainment until a 1,500-seat cinema opened in 1940. The Garrison Theatre was later created in a Nissen hut on the road between Lyness and Longhope, and other theatres were opened in Stromness and Kirkwall. Lyness also sported a church in a Nissen hut, St Ninian's (Episcopal), a Catholic church (another Nissen hut consecrated as the Church of St Thomas More), a

Fig. 73
Smoke rises from an oil tank hit during a bombing raid in Norway. Another bomb has landed in the water. The attack was carried out by aircraft from HMS Furious, *based at Scapa Flow.*

Church of Scotland, an officers' club, an RAF gym and a dance hall. The more humble but equally essential services were also represented: the base needed, for example, water, victualling, repair facilities, an education centre, a fire-fighting school, sewage and waste disposal, policing and laundry on a town scale – the laundry handled over 4,000 blankets per month. Interestingly, in view of the stock perception of military life, the Admiralty records say that Lyness acquired a dental surgery a year before a barber shop. The accommodation was nearly always spartan: the curved walls of the Nissen hut housing the officers' club enclosed a functional space furnished with small, square tables and upright wood and leather chairs on a bare wood floor, partly relieved by two sofas near the bar where waited the four unadorned barrels of beer and a shelf for bottles. The walls were painted a pale colour and someone kept vases of flowers in the windows.

The golf course Jellicoe had ordered built on Flotta to give his officers some

exercise was reclaimed and, as in the First World War, ships were given the responsibility to look after different parts of it. 'The *Valiant* was given one of the greens and a tee, and a couple of bunkers,' recalled Roddy Macdonald, 'and every time the ship was in harbour a working party went ashore. We also did the pier at Flotta. It was repaired, mostly by our diver and the gunner; the gunner was called Cuds and we knew the pier as Cuds's Pier'.

The NAAFI showed movies once a week, and eventually live entertainment came to feature. The Entertainment National Service Association (ENSA) staged variety concerts and among the stars who came to Scapa to cheer the troops were Gracie Fields, George Formby, Sybil Thorndike, Beatrice Lillie and Evelyn Laye. Yehudi Menuhin took his violin and played to the drifter and destroyer crews, anchored out on the water. On the Caithness side of the Firth, life was much the same except that the RAF stationed in Wick had to use ingenuity and local know-how to overcome the problem of their nearest urban centre being a 'dry town', a dilemma that most surmounted, it seems, with little difficulty.

Fig. 74 (previous pages) *A Junkers 88 bomber lies crippled in the stubble near Sandwick after being shot down on Christmas Day, 1940. This was the first German aircraft to fall victim to an American-built aircraft in the Second World War.*

Fig. 75 (above) *Two WAAFs of the Photographic Section, Skeabrae Air Station.*

In September 1938 Hetty Munro enlisted in one of the original county companies of the Women's Auxiliary Territorial Service (ATS) in Thurso. In the following May, the women were issued with their uniforms, which included a tartan skirt, and in September, at the start of the war, Hetty found herself one of eight clerks posted to Orkney – at that time considered an overseas posting – with the rank of Assistant Section Leader, something she defined as being equivalent to corporal. (Later in the war she was commissioned.) In her own words, she worked as 'a sort of head cook and bottle washer' in the General Staff of Brigadier, later Major General, Kemp, a job that brought the good fortune of knowing most of what went on. She enjoyed the work and the chance it presented to meet all kinds of people. Her first impression of Winston Churchill was less than flattering: 'a funny little fat, white man,' she wrote in her diary, 'sitting hunched up in a car wearing a dreadful naval cap with plain clothes – he looked like the owner of a "Saucy Sue" ready to take anyone for a trip at 6d a time'. This opinion did not, however, blind her to the Prime Minister's drive.

Fig. 76
The Seafire, the naval version of the Spitfire, proved to be too weakly constructed for the rigours of carrier operations, as this one from 894 Squadron after a crash landing on HMS Implacable *in November 1944 shows.*

Her diary records what it was like for the hundreds of young men and women, many away from home for the first time and thrown together in a perilous situation. Their resilience comes through: the jokes in the middle of danger and death, and the snatching of joy. 'Had a wonderful party at Tankerness House recently,' she recorded in the middle of 1940. 'Everyone was there and I managed to get out of uniform which gave me such a good feeling.' In June 1941, she wrote: 'After dinner Pier Groves arrived. He'd been chasing the *Bismarck* and had had a very exciting time in lots of ships. He'd also . . . spent a couple of days in Iceland – souvenirs of his visits there being lemons, cheese, smoked salmon and silk stockings.'

Fig. 77
Some of the staff aboard the depot ship HMS Dunluce Castle *in August 1943. This ex-Union Castle liner was about to be scrapped in 1939 when she was bought by the navy to be a depot ship in Scapa.*

Fig. 78
The switchboard in the Wee Fea telecommunications centre. Wee Fea is the name of the hill overlooking Lyness.

Fig. 79
The complement of Wrens who staffed the Wee Fea communications centre.

If there was one thing Scapa Flow could provide in abundance, it was open space. For many the long, stark horizons and the relative scarcity of people were a revelation and a delight. 'It was a magic place for me,' said Geoffrey Davies on the *Vasna*, 'quite tranquil – a high sky with those horizontal clouds, and summer light to read our letters on deck up until midnight.' Davies celebrated his twenty-first birthday in the Flow, and his messmates baked a cake for a high tea and gave him a tartan-covered volume of Burns. On their half-days ashore, he and his mates walked from Scapa pier into Kirkwall, calling on the way at an old-fashioned pub, with spittoons and sawdust, where drink was always a dram and a chaser, when they had any booze at all. Alternative outings were to town cafés or to some of Orkney's treasured archaeological sites such as Skara Brae.

Some of the experience of Scapa Flow was encapsulated in verse. One poem has entered the British folksong repertoire; a few of its verses are as follows:

This bloody town's a bloody cuss –
No bloody trains, no bloody bus,
And no one cares for bloody us –
In bloody Orkney.

Fig. 80
The telecommunications centre at Wee Fea, near Lyness.

The bloody roads are bloody bad,
The bloody folks are bloody mad,
They'd make the brightest bloody sad,
In bloody Orkney.

No bloody sport, no bloody games,
No bloody fun, the bloody dames
Won't even give their bloody names
In bloody Orkney.

Ascribed to a Captain Hamish Blair, this poem first appeared in the forces newspaper *The Orkney Blast*. Not everyone agreed with its sentiments. One anonymous rebuttal in the same organ stated:

I read a most distressing verse,
In accents bloody and so terse
That I produce one the reverse
Of this, our Orkney

We came up here with naught to lose,
For pleasure there is much to choose,
Especially if you want to booze,
In flowing Orkney

My seven days' leave I almost spurn,
With all those wasted hours to burn,
Before the moment of return,
To blessed Orkney.

Fig. 81 (previous page)
Two air mechanics working on the engine of a damaged Martinet at Twatt.

Fig. 82 (opposite)
Wrens, with a little help from a pet, removing apparatus from a Walrus seaplane at Twatt, March 1944.

Fig. 83
Lyness from the slopes of Wee Fea.

Another – called 'Orcadian Rhapsody' – celebrated the unusual place-names of the islands and began:

I have trodden the braes of Blinkbonny
And basked in the sun at Smoogro
I've meandered from Yarpha to Swannay
And danced with the pixies at Roo;

and ended:

All my life I shall never forget it,
The blessed Elysian plot,
The lure of Cockmurra and Ettit,
Of Cursiter, Youbell and Twatt.

The Orkney Blast was founded by Eric Linklater at the request of Major-General Kemp, to relieve the tedium afflicting the scattered troop detachments. It carried strip cartoons, stories, articles and news items and remained popular throughout its life, from the first issue on 17 January 1941, produced in a raging blizzard, until the end of the war. There were occasional censorship scares, such as when the name Skeabrae was mentioned and 'the entire [HQ] staff worked for hours to

Fig. 84
HMS Ophelia *in Hoy Sound. She carried out anti-submarine, escort and minesweeping duties.*

cut the word out of 2,000 copies',[78] a solution to the dilemma that gives some indication of how eagerly anticipated the weekly paper was. Linklater soon handed over the editor's chair to a London soldier, Private Jerry Mayer, who, after the war, remained in Orkney to edit the local paper, *The Orcadian*, until his retirement in 1983.

Fig. 85
A game of hockey in progress under the guns on the deck of a capital ship.

Fig. 86 (overleaf)
'It ain't half windy, mum.' A concert party on Shapinsay.

Exercises produced their own brand of humour – 'fun' in the opinion of Hetty Munro who was in the privileged position of being able to read the reports. One caused her considerable amusement: 'I think the prize was taken by the Battalion Commander who wrote that at Z hours and 30 minutes he "ordered there should be no more casualties as the RAMC orderlies were over-worked!!!"' [her exclamation points].

The Orkney islands are fertile and the strictures of wartime rationing were consequently less severe than back home. In the early days, however, the incomers had much to learn. As first lieutenant on the drifter *Lunar Bow*, Roddy Macdonald had the responsibility of feeding the crew. On patrol near Kirk Sound on the Sunday the war broke out, he found the larder empty, apart from

Fig. 87
Polish soldiers at Hatston.

unappetising emergency rations, and went ashore in the skiff to search for food. The Territorial Army depot in the nearest village had nothing to spare but told him about an old woman nearby, reputedly 'possessed of the evil eye and therefore unconcerned with the stricter aspects of Lord's Day observance' who might be worth asking. Indeed she was. She baked scones and bread for the seamen and allowed them to take some of her hens, provided they caught them themselves. 'Later we learned to barter firewood, which was scarce in Orkney, for mutton which was [abundant].'

The Orcadian noted in December 1941 that, although toys were scarce that Christmas, the civilians and service people in the islands were a lot better off than those elsewhere. Eggs were plentiful, and many a serviceman mailed a box to his relatives or, when going on leave, took some home with him. Ella Stephen helped with teas in a canteen in Palace Road, Kirkwall, and remembers the pancakes being gobbled up so quickly the cooks couldn't keep pace. Many a local family invited serving personnel to their home and fed them on the best of local meat and vegetables. In this way some lasting friendships were established and the visitors came to appreciate the quiet, reliable ways of their hosts who at first had displayed a reserve that must have puzzled and amused them – when Orkney gunners shot down a Junkers in 1940, they applauded rather than cheered!

Many Orcadians found employment in the ancillary services in support of the military. William Mowatt worked on the building of gunsites on Burray and, later, as a fisherman, sailed across from South Ronaldsay to John o'Groats with cargoes of lobsters – it was not unknown for him to see a submarine periscope poking from the waves in the Firth. One of my Caithness uncles was a sergeant in the Home Guard and kept hand grenades under his bed. In Kirkwall Ella Stephen's family owned the St Ola Hotel and, when it was taken over to provide accommodation for Fleet Air Arm officers, the premises were divided internally to leave quarters for the owners in one part. The Kirkwall and Queens Hotels were also commandeered, along with various premises in the harbour area. The ground floor of the Masonic Hall became a sick bay, the offices of the North of Scotland Steamship Company were turned into the headquarters of the base engineer, petty officers had a club on the first floor of the municipal library, the Temperance Hall became a recreation room and later a cinema, and a mail office was opened above Flett's shop in Bridge Street. HMS *Pyramus*, the shore-based contraband control station, was also sited in Kirkwall to examine merchant shipping and, at the height of its activity, as many as a hundred ships could be waiting in Kirkwall Bay.

The concentration of armed forces in Orkney in both wars brought much work for local contractors and merchants, and farmers also benefited from the demand for their produce, although at times they were stretched to cope, especially as much of the skilled labour force was away serving in other theatres of war. The imposition of restrictions on free movement – in the Second War, for example, the universal blackout was reinforced with a curfew which forbade anyone to be out after 11 p.m. without good reason – was often irksome and at times hated, but overall the people of the islands took things in their stride.

On Stroma, in the middle of the Pentland Firth, with a clear view of the main entrance to the Flow, Sutherland Manson observed and remembered the novelty war brought to his doorstep: 'The first convoy I can recall came

Fig. 88
The staff of The Orkney Blast.

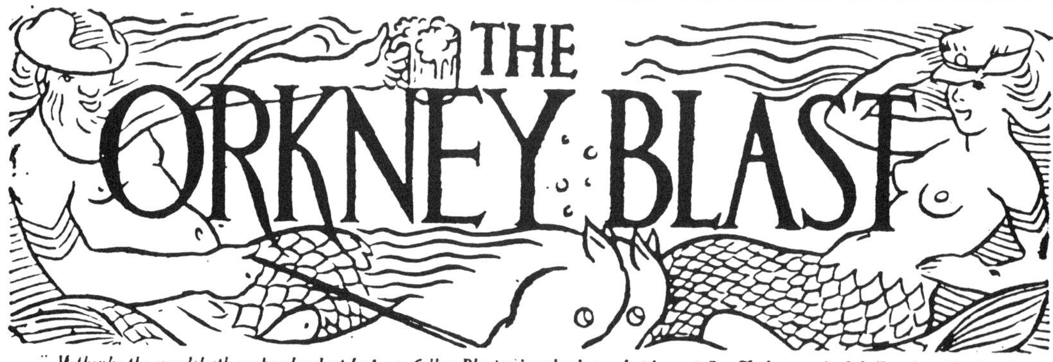

"Methinks the wind hath spoke aloud at land; a fuller Blast ne'er shook our battlements."—Shakespeare's Othello, Act II., Sc. I.

No. [illegible] PUBLISHED WEEKLY FOR H.M. FORCES STROMNESS, FRIDAY, JULY 11, 1941 PRICE THREEPENCE.

Gracie Fields for Orkney

DUE HERE NEXT WEEK

Bringing Artistes With Her

SOME few days ago the news flashed round the world that Gracie Fields, world-famous Rochdale-born star-comedienne, was "coming home."

Today THE BLAST is able to announce the glad tidings that "Our Gracie" will make in Orkney one of her first ENSA appearances. She is due here towards the end of next week and will remain for two days.

Major Haygarth, in charge of Entertainments in Orkney, yesterday told THE BLAST that Gracie would give shows in Orkney for two days during which she would make several appearances. Tickets will be apportioned to the various Services. The usual halls will not be used. Special larger premises are being utilised, so that a maximum number of troops will be able to see and hear Gracie.

MEMORIES FOR MANY

Troops who were stationed in France in the earlier days of the war will recall with pleasure Gracie's many appearances there. THE BLAST is able to state authoritatively that Gracie is bringing with her some of the artistes who appeared with her in France, and we are thus assured of receiving treats similar to those Gracie and her colleagues provided in France.

Arrangements for the tour, which has been organised by Mr Basil Dean, recently appointed Director of the National Services Entertainments by the Government, are in the very capable hands of Major Haygarth, who was responsible for all Gracie's shows in France.

Readers will recall that Gracie and her husband, film-director Monty Banks, left this country for America nearly a year ago.

It was natural that Gracie's departure from these shores should, at the time, arouse some controversy . . . even to the point of questions being asked in Parliament. Such was the penalty of fame.

And Gracie was hurt.

GRAND WORK IN AMERICA

Nevertheless during her stay on the other side of the Atlantic, Gracie gave innumerable shows, and not only won thousands of new friends . . . but, more important to us, thousands of invaluable dollars for the Allied war effort.

Before leaving this country Gracie promised to return to England to entertain the troops this Autumn.

That promise she is now faithfully keeping.

Gracie's still "doing her bit."

Once upon a time it was feared that illness had put an end to her stage career.

But Gracie's not the type to "go down easily."

She put up a splendid fight, and there was national rejoicing when her voice was once more heard in full song.

That's how we'll feel when she sings to us here.

Gracie's had a tough time. In the excitement of war there were many who momentarily misjudged her departure. [illegible] their too ready tongues.

At the time Gracie "took it" on that famous chin and with that great heart of smile.

(CONTINUED ON PAGE FOUR)

MARGARET LINDSAY, beautiful brunette, Warner Bros' star, who will be remembered for her work in "Cavalcade" and many other films, occupies the front page today, in our weekly feature of film and stage personalities.

BLAST GARDENS COMPETITION

Judging of Mainland Section Nears Completion

THE Judges of the Garden Competition, after a busy week of visits, have now completed their preliminary survey of the entries submitted, and have forwarded a preliminary report for publication.

The standard of entries varied very much, but in nearly every case the entries results were seen in gardens where the Officer Commanding Unit had taken a real and personal interest in the cultivation.

"The [illegible] effort, however, is the case of an isolated searchlight site situated on an exposed hill, in a heather moor.

Here, on a bare, wind-swept and rocky hillside, a magnificent little garden has been brought into being through the efforts of one man helped by nine others.

But for the plots had to be carried a considerable distance, and even when it was prepared for planting, protected by carefully built turf walls, the [illegible] was practically [illegible] [illegible] the troops that their efforts would be in vain. Far from this is the result, however.

"On this desolate site there now flourish some [illegible] hundred feet containing potatoes, cabbages, peas, broad beans, lettuces, radishes and onions, while at the hut entrance neatly built peat gardens and beds of flowers [illegible] beautifully.

NO. 1 HARLEY STREET

"Of a different type, and blessed with more of Nature's aid, is the garden of 'No. 1 Harley Street,' our medical friends in Stromness.

With soil of comparatively good quality, but which still required considerable preparation, the Unit, under the guidance of an expert gardener, has produced what must be one of the finest displays of vegetables in Orkney.

"Impressive is the area under cultivation, the neatness of the layout, and the advanced and strong state of the plants.

AMERICAN TROOPS IN ICELAND

Nazis Reach Stalin Line

BY "THE BLAST" MILITARY CORRESPONDENT

This week, THE BLAST Military Correspondent welcomes the news that the U.S.A. are sending troops to relieve our men at present in Iceland. The theatres of war in Russia, Abyssinia and Syria are also dealt with in the light of present information.

THE news has just come in that American troops are being sent to Iceland. They are to reinforce our own troops for the time being, and finally to take over the defences altogether, thus relieving our troops for service elsewhere.

This news is very welcome, for the more trained troops that we have at our disposal the better: it is also rather a setback for Hitler who must have had his eye on Iceland as a good jumping-off place for attacks on shipping and the Western Hemisphere.

There was always the possibility of an attack on Iceland while we had troops there, but an attack on the island when defended by Americans would mean that America would certainly enter the war, and it is unlikely that Hitler would wish to take such a risk, except as a last resort. The change will also be very welcome to the troops in Iceland, most of whom will have been up there for over a year.

Russian Defences Holding

The Russian war is now well on in its third week and, so far, no startling change has taken place.

True, the Germans have made advances along most of the front, but in the main, no German troops have crossed the real Russian frontier. A report has been received from German sources that at one point their troops have come up against the Stalin line. This line appears, from accounts, to be really a deep defended locality in which full use has been made of natural hazards such as hills, rivers and woods.

This line, if manned by sufficient troops, should prove a severe stumbling block to the German advance.

The Germans themselves are not expecting a lightning victory, as is shown by the remarks made by their Military Attache in Ankara who said that the campaign against Russia would take at least two or three months to complete. This is the first time that the Germans have admitted that they will take some time over one of their campaigns.

Abyssinian Campaign Ended

The Abyssinian campaign has now, to all intents and purposes been completed. There is a force at Gondar and a few stragglers in the wild country sector west of Assab, but apart from that the country is quiet again. It may be said by some people that the Abyssinian show has been going on far too long already, but it must be remembered that for the last two or three months the rains have been on, and that, during the rains, it is practically impossible to do any fighting.

Our forces have, in fact, made some amazing advances through torrential rain and over roads which were practically rivers, but any rapid progress has been impossible.

Our progress in Syria continues slowly. We have now taken most of the southern part and are closing in on Beirut. We have also a column advancing along the boundary between Syria and Turkey with the presumed intention of capturing Aleppo. Progress in this campaign has also been slow, but with Germany fully engaged in the campaign against Russia, it is unlikely that she will be able to send any assistance to the Vichy forces.

Another effort most worthy of note is the garden produced by a Supply Unit in East Mainland.

Here, in the short period of six to eight weeks, a most unusual garden of vegetables has been cultivated, while flower beds border the entrance roadway and hut entrances, not to mention a vegetable marrow bed and a turf-wall protected area for late cabbages. At this and many other sites the season's crop has already proved most useful.

COWS ENJOY GOOD MEAL

The above noteworthy examples are typical of the better entries.

Some newly arrived Units have come to sites previously uncultivated, but are making the best of a belated start.

"One unfortunate Unit had the tragic experience of finding cows calmly munching all their newly planted cabbages just as the latter were beginning to thrive.

"In more than one case the Engineers are blamed for digging trenches through newly-sown plots.

But such trifles as these have not daunted our enthusiasts and even the poorest result deserves the credit of having made the effort—often against seemingly impossible odds."

It is hoped to publish the results of the Mainland Section in our Stop Press, and a full report of the winning schemes next week.

Fig. 89 (opposite)
The masthead of The Orkney Blast.

Fig. 90 (left)
A Gordon Highlander poses while an AT seems more engrossed in The Orkney Blast.

Fig. 91 (overleaf)
The drifter Inverboyndie.

through the Firth on 14 August 1940. Subsequently such assemblies of shipping were a familiar sight, consisting at times of from fifty to sixty vessels of all shapes and sizes, which might even include the odd Great Lakes trader pressed into transatlantic service. Initially escorting vessels were few in number, a destroyer and two armed trawlers perhaps, but this situation was improved.'

After the alarms and excitement of the first year of the war, the men on the anti-aircraft batteries passed their time waiting for attacks that never came and had to put up with endless practice sessions and exercises to keep them on their toes and, as one man put it, 'Just to ensure that every man woke up at least once a

11
INVERBOYNDIE

Fig. 92
The Lunar Bow (*line drawing by Roddy Macdonald*).

month, the Orkney barrage was fired'.[79] The Pioneer Corps were busier – they had to build and maintain the encampments and installations, by no means a cushy number in the northern winter. Then there were base workers: ship repairmen and any number of clerks, orderlies, cooks and storekeepers. A floating dock big enough to accommodate a destroyer arrived in August 1940, just a couple of months before it was required to take in HMS *Mendip* after she blew off her stern with one of her own depth charges. AFD 12, as the dock was termed, had a busy existence and by the time she was towed away to the Far East in June 1945 she had docked 343 ships.

A fleet of small craft acted as tenders to the capital ships, as messenger boats and ferries, and worked to maintain the defensive booms. Some of these – the drifters and armed trawlers, with mixed crews of some navy regulars or reservists among the ex-fishermen – might find themselves patrolling or minesweeping in monotonous regularity and could spend days at sea within sight of the shore but without setting a foot on land.

The *Lunar Bow*, the *Belfast*'s tender, was a typical drifter, with high bows and a tall funnel that belched black smut-filled smoke from her coal-fired boilers. The wardroom, wireless office and magazine were squeezed into the fish-hold, and the open bridge exposed the officer of the watch to the prevailing wind, and also to showers of cinders when it was a fair one. The funnel often became red-hot but, wrote Roddy Macdonald, 'it was not considered polite when in close company to make toast on other ships' funnels'.

'Except for the bloodshot eyes of the officer of the watch,' he continued, 'the drifters had no means of detecting submarines [one of their main duties

Fig. 93
Captain Macdonald's pipe band playing on the flight deck of HMS Implacable *in Scapa Flow. The captain also had a piper play for dinner.*

early in the war]. The two depth charges were a menace. The ship was so slow that, had we fired them, they would have removed the stern. We mounted a three-pounder gun and even carried out a practice shoot. The first salvo was a hit but this was not surprising as the target was a hundred-foot cliff. A large section of rock descended into the sea with a noise like thunder, while we steamed away trying not to look like a very small ship that had recently caused a landslide.

'Being primitive, it was difficult to be conventional even in what, as everyone knows, was a conventional war. On one occasion in a thick fog we made contact with our relief ship by playing hopeful airs on the bagpipes. Another ship claimed that it had developed a high-powered cheese which glowed in the dark and could be smelt two miles downwind with the lid off. But in the main we relied on our anchor which to this day is the most effective navigational device invented. It was certainly the solution when the tidal stream flowed strongly. Only anchoring could prevent our progress being an undignified one in the wrong direction.'

The original design for the anti-submarine booms called for a single line of net

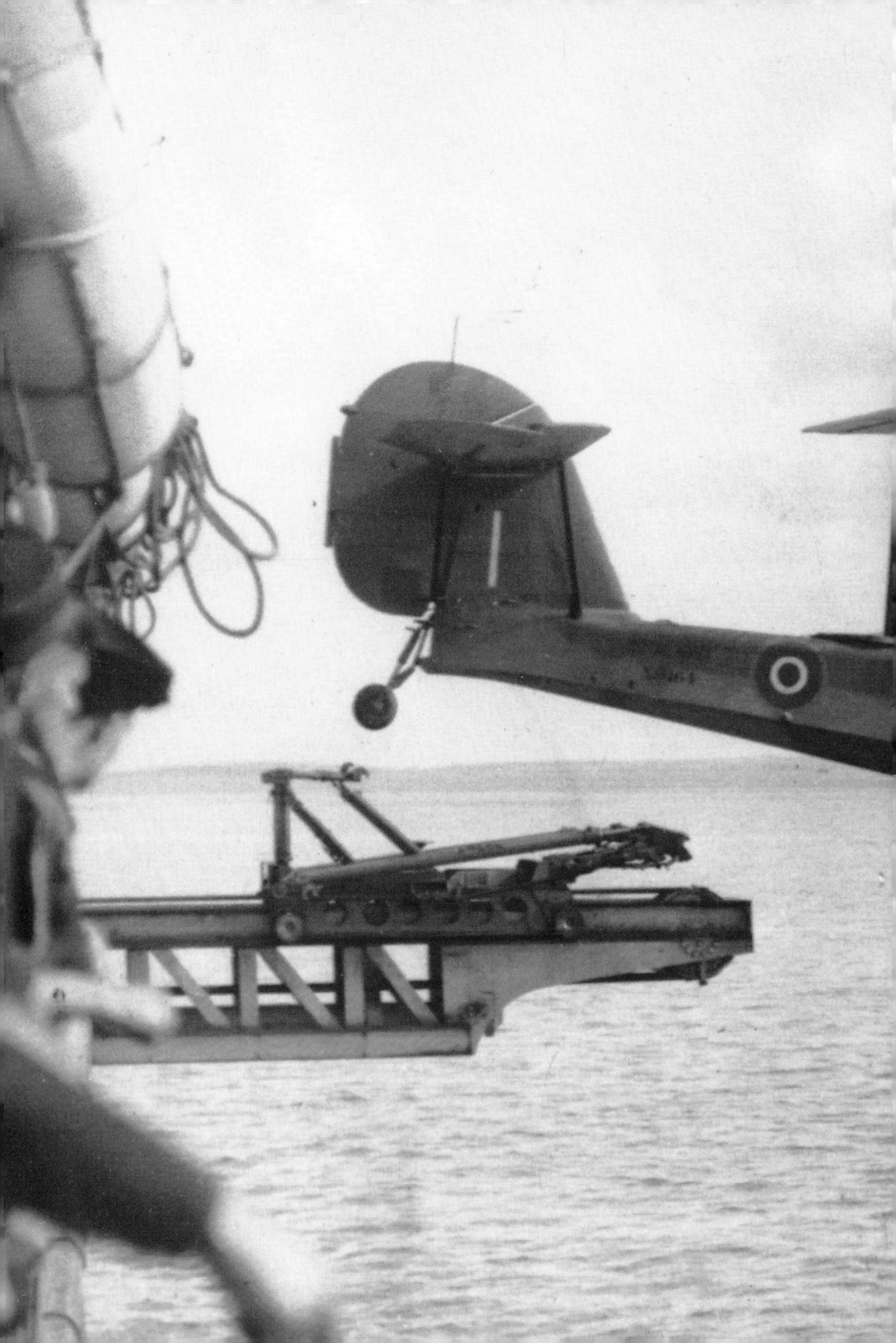

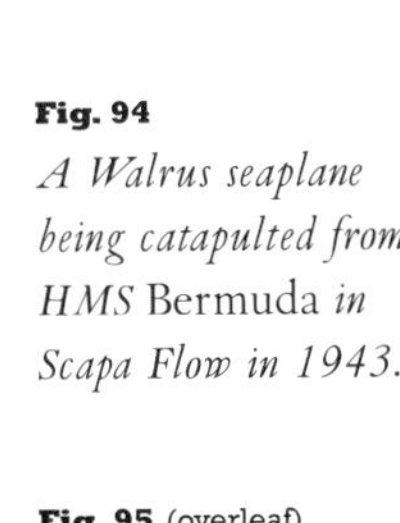

Fig. 94
A Walrus seaplane being catapulted from HMS Bermuda *in Scapa Flow in 1943.*

Fig. 95 (overleaf)
The Walrus being hoisted aboard HMS Bermuda *after landing on the sea alongside.*

Fig. 96
A Walrus seaplane arriving at the Hatston slipway.

made from three-inch wire rope woven with an eight-foot mesh but eventually all the booms were given a double wall of net. After the penetration by *U-47*, a fourth boom, between Hunda and the east point of the Calf of Flotta, was added in November 1940 to the three already in place. The care of the booms was a dirty, rough job but the integrity of the walls of wire lay at the heart of the Flow's defence system. During the war, sixteen boom vessels with their distinctive horned prows, twelve trawlers and 1,100 officers and men were devoted to boom duties.

They had to cope with a continual series of accidents and collisions. For example, on 6 November 1940, it was recorded that 'HM Destroyer *Electra* collided with HMBDV *Barnwell*, the senior or closing gate vessel at Hoxa boom, and carried away both closing wires and the port quarter moorings. The gate could thus not be closed. HMBVs *Barlow* and *Barbican* were immediately sent and repairs effected. *Barlow* resplicing the closing wires and *Barbican* relaying port quarter moorings. Repairs were completed on the same day.'[80]

Anyone who has tried to splice three-inch wire rope on a heaving November sea will know what had to be done. Sometimes the repairs had to wait. On Sunday

17 December 1944, HMS *Devonshire* fouled the boom and carried away a piece of it. HMBVs *Barglow* and *Falconet* came to the scene but 'owing to heavy gales and rough sea were unable to do more than stand by until the following day. Hard work on the part of the ship's riggers and good seamanship by the CO resulted in *Devonshire* being cleared . . . on the Monday. HMBV *Falconet* stood by to assist whilst Metal Industries divers burnt away the A/T nets fouling her propellers.'

Days or weeks might creep by without much of anything happening but then the unforeseen would burst into the lives of the servicemen, so that no one was allowed to forget for too long the reason for their presence. Scapa Flow was the setting for many significant events. Pilot Officer Michael Suckling, on patrol from Wick in a long-range Spitfire, photographed the battleship *Bismarck* in a fjord near Bergen on 21 May 1941. The pride of the German navy, the *Bismarck* – 41,700 tons, capable of twenty-eight knots and carrying eight fifteen-inch guns in her main armament – was the most powerful warship of her time. A second reconnaissance flight on the evening of the following day, this time from Hatston, in a Maryland AR717 bomber flown by Squadron Commander Noel Goddard, revealed that she and her escort, the *Prinz Eugen*, were no longer in the fjord. Admiral Sir John Tovey, who had taken over as C-in-C of the Home Fleet in December 1940, had already ordered his two fastest heavy ships, HMS *Hood* and HMS *Prince of Wales*, to sail from Scapa at full speed to reinforce the cruisers patrolling in the Denmark Strait between Iceland and Greenland. HMS *King George V* and the carrier HMS *Victorious*, with some cruisers and destroyers, sailed on a more westerly course. It was vital to find the *Bismarck* before she broke through into the North Atlantic to threaten the Atlantic convoys on which Britain depended.

Just before six o'clock on 24 May, as dawn was breaking, the *Hood* and the *Prince of Wales* spotted their prey and the four ships opened fire on each other. Hit by a plunging shell that drilled through into a magazine, the *Hood* blew up and sank with the loss of all her complement except three. The *Prince of Wales* under heavy fire broke off her own attack but not before two of her shots had damaged the *Bismarck*'s fuel tanks. The German battleship managed to elude her pursuers for a further two days but finally, on the twenty-fifth, making for Brest, she succumbed to concentrated attack by the Royal Navy.

In the early years of the war, German intelligence had made considerable progress in breaking the ciphers used by the Royal Navy. Although by the autumn of 1940 the Admiralty suspected that the security of their signals had been compromised, the full extent of the enemy's penetration was not realised until after 1945. It was also true of course that British intelligence was busily

Fig. 97
A Sunderland flying boat under tow.

working to break German codes. In May 1941, the corvette *Aubretia*, one of the escorts on an Atlantic convoy, forced *U-110* to surface and her crew to abandon ship in haste. A boarding party from the destroyer *Bulldog* retrieved from the U-boat an intact Enigma machine, the heart of the German coded signalling system, and brought it to Scapa in a major stroke of luck for the intelligence service.

The Flow may have become a place of numbing tedium for many but the sailors and airmen returning there from hazardous operations appreciated its tranquillity. When Charles McAra first saw Scapa, in 1940, he was an Ordinary Seaman on the destroyer HMS *Cottesmore*: 'a desolate place . . . covered in January snow and scourged day and night by bitterly cold winter days . . . I felt that if we could cope as we pitched and tossed and rolled and yawed in the stabbing seas off the Orkneys, we could probably manage anywhere.' By 1942, when he was an officer on a minesweeper, the bleakness 'only served to make all the more moving the sight of all the grey ships . . . if they were lucky, the place to which they returned'.[81]

★

Fig. 98
The reconnaissance photo taken on 21 May 1941 by Pilot Officer Michael Suckling of the Bismarck *at anchor in a fjord near Bergen.*

McAra was thinking of the Arctic convoys, the notorious PQ and QP series that ran between September 1941 and the end of 1942. The convoys continued until the end of the war but the code designation changed in late 1942 to JW and RA. The escorts usually left Scapa to rendezvous with the merchant ships on the Icelandic coast before tackling the grim passage around the North Cape to some dour Russian port. In this Allied effort to supply the Soviet Union, ninety-one merchant ships, two cruisers and seventeen other warships were sunk and 2,669

Fig. 99
A four-inch gun crew on HMS Suffolk *grab some sleep beside their gun while on patrol in northern waters in June 1941.*

seamen lost their lives.[82] The most fateful voyage was PQ17, in July 1942, when alarm over the presence of German capital ships led the Admiralty to order the escort to withdraw and the convoy to scatter, with the result that U-boats and aircraft had a free hand: twenty-three out of the thirty-four ships in the convoy went to the bottom of the Arctic.[83]

In April 1942, the Flow welcomed the first United States Navy Task Force, TF 39, later re-designated TF 99, to join the war in Europe when the new battleship USS *Washington*, the carrier USS *Wasp*, two heavy cruisers *Tuscaloosa* and *Wichita*, and six destroyers sailed in through Hoxa Sound. The voyage across the Atlantic had been marred by a curious incident: the commander, Rear-Admiral John W. Wilcox, had been lost overboard from the *Washington*. Wilcox's death has never been completely explained but it is thought he suffered a heart attack and fell from the ship in heavy seas; his body was spotted in the water but an extensive search failed to recover it. British officers invited to dine in the American wardrooms were astonished by the quality and quantity of the food, but puzzled by the informality of the discipline. The Yanks proved to be a source of rare goodies in the way of eatables and some social diversion. The pre-war output from Hollywood had left the British public with a somewhat starry-eyed view of America, and perhaps this was reinforced by the fact that Douglas Fairbanks Jr. was serving on the *Washington* as a liaison officer.

In an exercise on 1 May, the *King George V* collided with the destroyer *Punjabi* and cut her in two. The *Washington*, coming up fast, could not avoid the sinking destroyer and passed between her two halves. Exploding depth charges caused only minor damage to the American ship; and fortunately most of the *Punjabi*'s crew, including her captain, were saved by other destroyers. The American ships were a welcome reinforcement for escort duties and some remained with the Home Fleet until the autumn, by which time Tovey had the new battleships HMS *Howe* and HMS *Duke of York* at his disposal. The *Wasp* was transferred in April to the Mediterranean to ferry aircraft to Malta; later, in the Pacific in September, she was torpedoed and sunk by a Japanese submarine.

Fig. 100 (overleaf) *HMS* Hood *anchored in a tranquil Scapa Flow.*

The role of the Home Fleet as a strategic reserve for operations virtually anywhere in the Atlantic and the Mediterranean meant that ships were continually being withdrawn from Scapa for service elsewhere, leaving Tovey at times without sufficient carrier power. Further American attachments ameliorated this situation. In October 1943, the carrier USS *Ranger* took part in attacks on shipping on the Norwegian coast, flying off her Dauntless dive bombers, Avengers and Wildcats to damage and sink vessels in the Bodø roadstead.

Sir Bruce Fraser replaced Sir John Tovey as C-in-C of the Home Fleet in May 1943. The battle-cruiser *Scharnhorst*, threatening the Russian convoys from her base in Altenfjord, was lured into combat with a superior British force, led by Fraser on HMS *Duke of York*, on Boxing Day 1943 and sunk, in the engagement named the Battle of the North Cape. The sinking of the *Scharnhorst* left only one major German ship in Norwegian waters, the *Tirpitz*, slightly larger than the *Bismarck* and a formidable threat to the convoys.

It took a long and considerable effort to remove this danger. Newly built, the *Tirpitz* slipped from the Baltic to Trondheim in January 1942. In March she ventured out to threaten convoy PQ12 but torpedo-bombers flown off from the *Victorious* in the vicinity of the Lofoten Islands failed to harm her. The Admiralty also attempted to neutralise her with midget submarines: the four-man X-class craft were developed specifically to sneak into guarded anchorages to attack ships such as the *Tirpitz*. In a test, the X-craft penetrated the Scapa Flow defences 'with no trouble at all and surfaced in the Flow', according to

Vernon Coles, the engine room artificer on one, an achievement much to the chagrin of the defenders.[84] Rumours of the Germans having such craft and the memory of the fate of the *Royal Oak* added to the defenders' worries. Six X-craft went after the *Tirpitz* in September 1943 and succeeded in disabling her sufficiently to prevent her escaping from Norwegian waters. Fleet Air Arm Barracuda bombers struck at the battleship in her haven in Kaafjord in April 1944 but failed to cause her lasting harm. Finally, after a further series of attacks by different means, in November 1944 RAF Lancasters of the Dambusters squadron bombed her and caused her to capsize at her moorings.

As soon as the enquiry into the sinking of the *Royal Oak* had pinpointed the likely route the enemy had used to break into the Flow, it became apparent that blockships would not be enough to prevent any similar future incursion. The only way to ensure no U-boat would ever again creep between the islands was to seal the gaps completely. The decision to dam the channels with what are now famous as the Churchill Barriers was finally taken in the autumn of 1939.

At any other time, the idea might have been dismissed as absurdly ambitious and expensive but the country was at war, fighting for her life, and other considerations were secondary. In fact, before the First World War, in May 1912, the possibility of permanently sealing the eastern channels had been considered but rejected as too costly and too difficult. After his visit at that time, the Director of Works from the War Office wrote that, for example Kirk Sound, 39 feet deep at low water during spring tides and with currents of eight knots, could be blocked by 'large blocks of stone tipped pell-mell, starting from the mainland and working straight across to Lamb Holm'.[85] The cheaper option of sinking blockships had been chosen in 1914.

The strong tidal currents through Kirk Sound, Skerry Sound, Weddel Sound and Water Sound – at the flood, the incoming surge banked up over the blockships – presented a tremendous challenge to the Admiralty engineer-in-chief, Sir Arthur Whitaker, and his assistants. After surveys and tests with a scale model at Manchester University, the contract for the momentous undertaking was awarded to Balfour Beatty. The liner *Almanzora*, accompanied by two tugs and a fleet of Thames barges, arrived off the village of Holm on 10 May 1940 to provide a floating base for equipment and manpower; and work began on what one lorry driver termed 'filling in the bleeding sea'.[86]

Piers, encampments and workyards – with railway lines, quarries and overhead cableways – sprang up on the islets of Lamb Holm and Glims Holm, and on the larger island of Burray. Convoys of lorries carried rocks for dumping in steel cages and gradually the race with the tide proceeded. By the end of 1941 considerable progress had been made but the retention of a sufficient workforce in the face of requirements elsewhere for the war effort was posing problems

Fig. 101
King George VI climbing aboard HMS Victorious *on a visit to Scapa Flow in May 1944.*

Fig. 102 (overleaf)
HMS Suffolk *on patrol among sea ice.*

Fig. 103 *The cruiser HMS* Newfoundland *on patrol.*

for the engineers about to tackle the damming of the deeper stretches of the Sounds.

This shortage of labour was solved, as is now widely known, by the shipping to Orkney of 600 Italian prisoners of war. This unusual reinforcement arrived in January 1942, landing at Warebanks Pier on Burray from a steamer. The POWs lived in camps and worked in squads, under guard and the direction of the

engineers. Unmistakable in their appearance – apart from the obvious difference in language, they wore large red discs on their clothes – the Italians were accepted by the locals and, on the whole, proved a willing and hard-working crowd. At the start, however, some among them were sceptical of their new role and protested that their employment on defences was in contravention of the Geneva Convention. In February the POWs refused to work; the authorities

Fig. 104
The Q Class destroyer, HMS Quiberon *steaming past the cliffs of Hoy en route to Scapa Flow in 1942. A year later she was transferred to the Royal Australian Navy.*

Fig. 105 (opposite, top)
Seamen, dressed for Arctic weather, on the deck of an aircraft carrier.

Fig. 106 (opposite, bottom)
The crew of HMS Berkshire, *an Auk-class minesweeper built in Houston, Texas, as the* Tourmaline *and transferred to the Royal Navy in 1943 under Lease-Lend.*

retaliated by placing them on a restricted, punishment diet. The 'troublemakers' among the prisoners were finally taken away and the remainder were reassured by a conciliatory and sympathetic commander that they were in no danger from being close to a naval base and that the work was for the benefit of local people – the defensive Barriers became civilian causeways.

Some of the Italians remained in Orkney until after the war, others left towards the end of 1944. By this time, they had won over the hearts of their captors. The capitulation of Italy as an enemy power in September 1943 had altered their situation – they were no longer prisoners, they received some pay in sterling and their living conditions improved. They took part in local pursuits and left a much prized tangible monument to their presence in the form of a chapel on the north shore of Lamb Holm. This ingenious structure – a simple Nissen hut transformed by a decorative gable and fittings of great beauty improvised from wrought iron, bathroom tiles and pieces of scrap – attracts many visitors. It was built under the guiding hand of one prisoner, an artist named Domenico Chiocchetti, who returned to Orkney to carry out some repairs and maintenance on his creation before his death in May 1999.

The effort 'to fill in the sea' gradually won success – the first of the barriers

Fig. 107
The American carrier USS Wasp *joined the Home Fleet in March 1942. Two months later, she was transferred to the Pacific where she was torpedoed in a Japanese attack in September 1942.*

Fig. 108 (overleaf)
A Gloster Gladiator, piloted by Captain H. St John Fancourt, lands on USS Wasp *in the Flow in May 1942.*

Fig. 109
A squadron of Devastator dive bombers crewed by American airmen being inspected at Hatston. The Orkney airfield was used for training.

71·F·23

broke the surface in June 1942[87] and by the end of that year Scapa Flow was safe from easterly assault. The causeway between Glims Holm and Burray was complete by the summer of 1943 and, by August that year, a man could walk dryshod and in safety from the mainland to Lamb Holm. Once the ribbon of rock and concrete bolsters was firmly in place, the sides were strengthened with cladding and a lane of tarmac was laid on the top.

The figures for material used, as recorded in the Admiralty files, give some indication of the effort expended in making the highways across the Sounds: 522,330 cubic yards of rock and 117,724 steel bolster nets, with 34,384 five-ton, 15,036 ten-ton and 2,206 eight-ton concrete blocks.

The roads built across the Barriers were officially opened to civilian traffic on 10 May 1945 by the First Sea Lord, Admiral A.V. Alexander, in a ceremony at Cara. The cost was given as £2 million and ten lives had been lost in the work.[88] *The Orcadian* described the First Sea Lord as being in high spirits and the weather as 'gloriously fine'. To music by the band of the Gordon Highlanders, Admiral Alexander cut the red, white and blue ribbon with a pair of scissors handed to him by G.G. Nicol, the engineer in the charge of the project. He went on later in the day to visit other parts of the Scapa Flow complex and enjoyed a tumultuous reception from 1,000 servicemen and women in the cinema at Lyness. Alexander

Fig. 110 (opposite) *American ground crew load ammunition belts into a Devastator dive bomber at Hatston.*

Fig. 111 (above) *Lieutenant Jean-Paul Fournier and a Wren enjoying a flight in a Sikorsky R-4 helicopter, one of the first such aircraft seen in Britain.*

Fig. 112 (overleaf) *American bombers flying east from USS* Ranger *towards the rising sun and the Norwegian coast in the strike on enemy shipping at Bodö in October 1943.*

Fig. 113 (previous pages) *The crew of HMS* Belfast *cheering the return of USS* Ranger *after she took part in air strikes on the Norwegian coast.*

Fig. 114 (above) *Carrying a squadron of Albacores, HMS* Victorious, *a 23,000-ton Illustrious class carrier built in 1941, heads from Scapa Flow to Iceland.*

thanked them for their six years of labour. We can hope that the Italians felt that day that they too had done a good job.

The war in Europe ended with VE Day on 8 May 1945. Three days before, the navy had launched its last attack – a carrier strike on a U-boat base at Kilbotn, north-west of Narvik. The military force around Scapa Flow had by then dwindled to a fraction of its former size as activity at the airfields was gradually wound down. The balloon barrage had been taken south to protect London in June 1944, and the evacuation of surplus personnel was already underway. In a quiet reprise of events in 1918, some U-boats made their way to Longhope to surrender. The *Iron Duke* was towed at last to the breakers' yard. On Monday 2 December 1946, the last Royal Navy officer left Kirkwall, after the formal closure of the naval base in the island capital the previous Saturday[89] (though a small navy presence was to remain until the final closing of the Scapa Flow base in 1957). At the same time, the two airfields of Skeabrae and Twatt were sold. The three navy establishments – HMS *Pleiades* (water transport), HMS *Proserpine* (base services) and HMS *Pomona* (boom defence) – were shrunk into one, retaining the name *Pomona*.

Metal Industries resumed its unfinished business with the battle-cruiser *Derfflinger* which had passed the duration upside down, under the care of a small gang of men who lived in a hut on her hull, and she was towed to Rosyth in 1946 for breaking up. Metal Industries closed its Lyness base in 1947 and, in 1956, sold its interest in the scuttled German fleet to Arthur Nundy of Nundy (Marine Metals) Ltd. Some more ships were broken up where they lay but no more were raised.

Fig. 115
A gun crew on HMS Port Quebec. *The picture was probably taken in June 1940. Originally a cargo liner, the* Port Quebec *was taken over by the Royal Navy in 1939 from a Sunderland firm and fitted out as a mine-layer. In 1943 the navy bought her and converted her to be a repair ship, renaming her* Deer Sound. *She returned to being a cargo vessel after the war.*

The navy continued to call. John Walling arrived in the Flow in the summer of 1949 as a cadet on HMS *Devonshire*; she stayed for a week or so, while the cadets painted the ship before the onward cruise to Scandinavia. Now a lieutenant commander in charge of a division of junior seamen on HMS *Vanguard*, Roddy Macdonald took some of them sailing in the Flow and landed on a small island. 'It was raining like mad,' he remembered. 'The boys enjoyed hunting rabbits by smoking them out of their holes with burning newspaper, and built a bonfire. On the following day, when we left harbour, looking back we could see smoke appearing from the island'. The captain said: 'Strange. That island appears to be on fire.' 'Oh really, sir?' murmured the non-committal lieutenant commander. On that occasion, the engineering commander on the *Vanguard* was forbidden from attempting to climb the Old Man of Hoy with a party of stokers. In June 1954, the *Vanguard* became the last battleship to enter Scapa Flow. Sightseers could take advantage of special trips on the *St Ola* – 12s 6d return and children half price – to view the Home Fleet on a Sunday afternoon.[90]

The final closing ceremony at Lyness – in March 1957 – was a low-key affair. After everything Scapa Flow represented, some thought it was grudgingly meagre. The only naval ship detailed to be present was a boom defence vessel, HMS *Barleycorn*, along with two oil tankers. It is tempting to guess what the

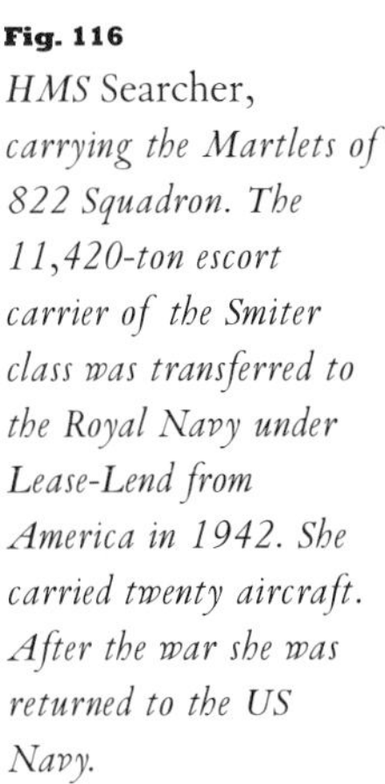

Fig. 116
HMS Searcher, *carrying the Martlets of 822 Squadron. The 11,420-ton escort carrier of the Smiter class was transferred to the Royal Navy under Lease-Lend from America in 1942. She carried twenty aircraft. After the war she was returned to the US Navy.*

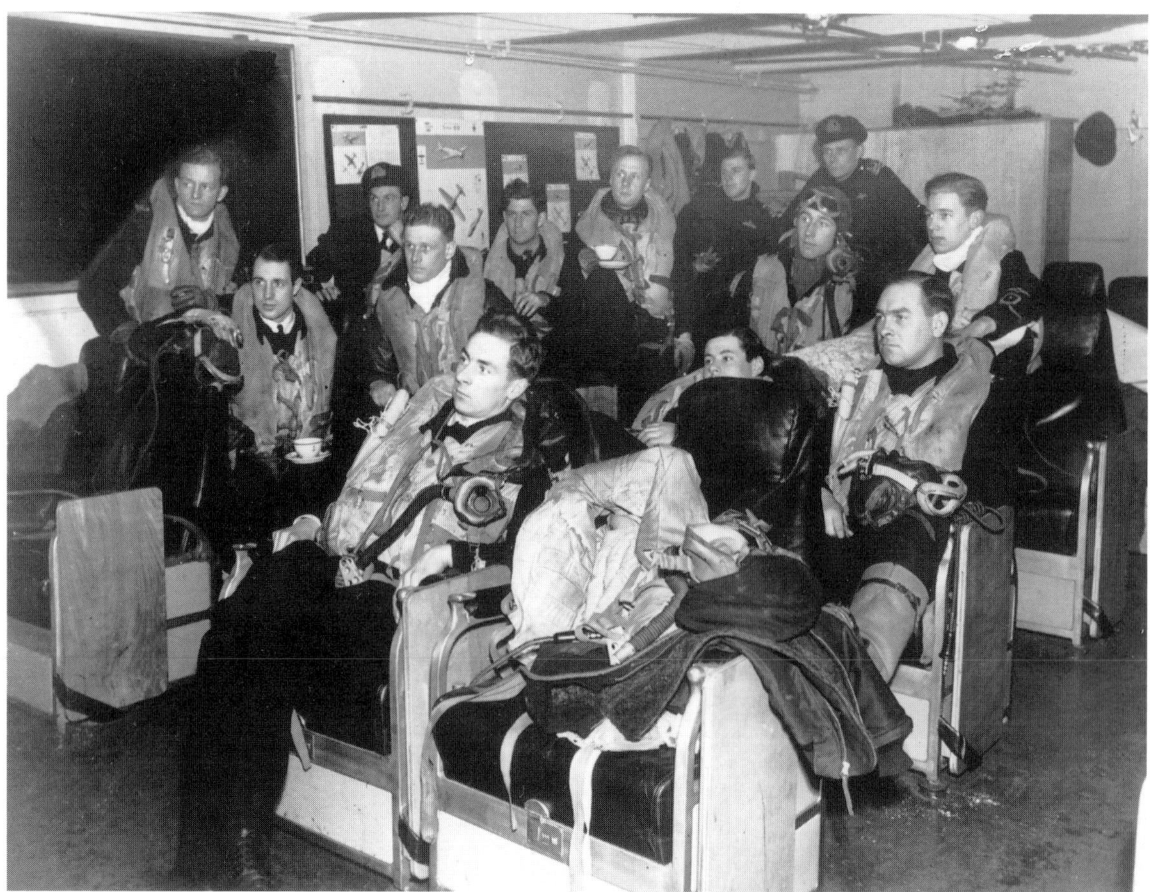

Fig. 117
Pilots of 822 Squadron being briefed on HMS Searcher *for an operation over Norway in 1943. The man whose head only is visible, 'Ned Kelly' Edney, was shot down and killed.*

Fig. 118 (opposite)
HMS King George V *executing a turn. The seaplane has come down near her port quarter. The 35,000-ton battleship was built in 1940 and was broken up in 1958.*

Flotta correspondent of the *Orkney Herald* who watched the navy steam in proud array into the Flow in 1909 would have made of it.

The Orcadian called it 'a day of poignant memories' when at sunset on Friday 29 March the White Ensign was lowered for the last time.[91] It was a grey, cold day with a snell, gusting wind. Close to 200 local people joined the forces to watch and remember. Rear-Admiral Sir Patrick Macnamara had already left and was unable to participate for 'health reasons and duty' but his wife, who like her husband had fallen in love with the stark beauty of Orkney was there, watching 'rather sadly' in the opinion of the journalist. Macnamara had commanded the anchorage in the last years of the war and his home had been Mill House in Mill Bay, where he kept two spaniels called Scapa and Flow.[92] The Lord Lieutenant of Orkney was also unable to be present. The most senior naval officer to attend was Captain A.J.M. Milne-Home, chief of staff to Flag Officer Scotland. The army was represented by a TA detachment from 861 (Independent) LAA Battery RA under their commander, Captain Affleck Thomson.

The resident naval officer, Commander C.C.S. Mackenzie, made a speech. He said that the formal dissolution of the base would not kill the affection in the

hearts of two generations of the Royal Navy for the place, an affection that, in his opinion, was growing warmer in retrospect than it ever was during winter nights in the Flow. Captain Milne-Home admitted in his address that he had mixed feelings, his personal attitude vying with the official one dictated by government policy. He had served here during the war, he said, and the name of Scapa Flow had a kind of mystical significance. He thanked the people of Orkney for helping to make it 'probably the finest naval base in the world'.

As the gloaming deepened and the cold wind blew in from the misty sea, the local minister offered prayers. After the crowd murmured 'Amen', the bubbling, melancholy note of a curlew echoed across the hills. The bugler played 'Sunset' as the White Ensign was lowered by the youngest crewman from the *Barleycorn*, nineteen-year-old Ordinary Seaman Ronald Henry. The most senior seaman, CPO Harry Berry, with twenty-six years' service, lowered the paying-off pennant, 226 feet long, one foot for every month in commission plus the length of the ship, in this case taken to be one of the MFVs, the drifters who had faithfully tended their larger sisters. It was, *The Orcadian* correspondent noted, the final moments for what had been in its heyday the greatest naval anchorage in the world with an anti-aircraft defence that could bring thirty to forty guns to bear on any patch of sky above it. Then two TA pipers played a lament, and the order 'March Off Parade' was given. There was a dance in the evening but by that time most of the visitors had gone.

Fig. 119 (opposite) *HMS* King George V.

Fig. 120 (above) *700 Squadron with a Sea Otter aircraft at Twatt airfield, taken in March 1944 before the disbanding of the squadron.*

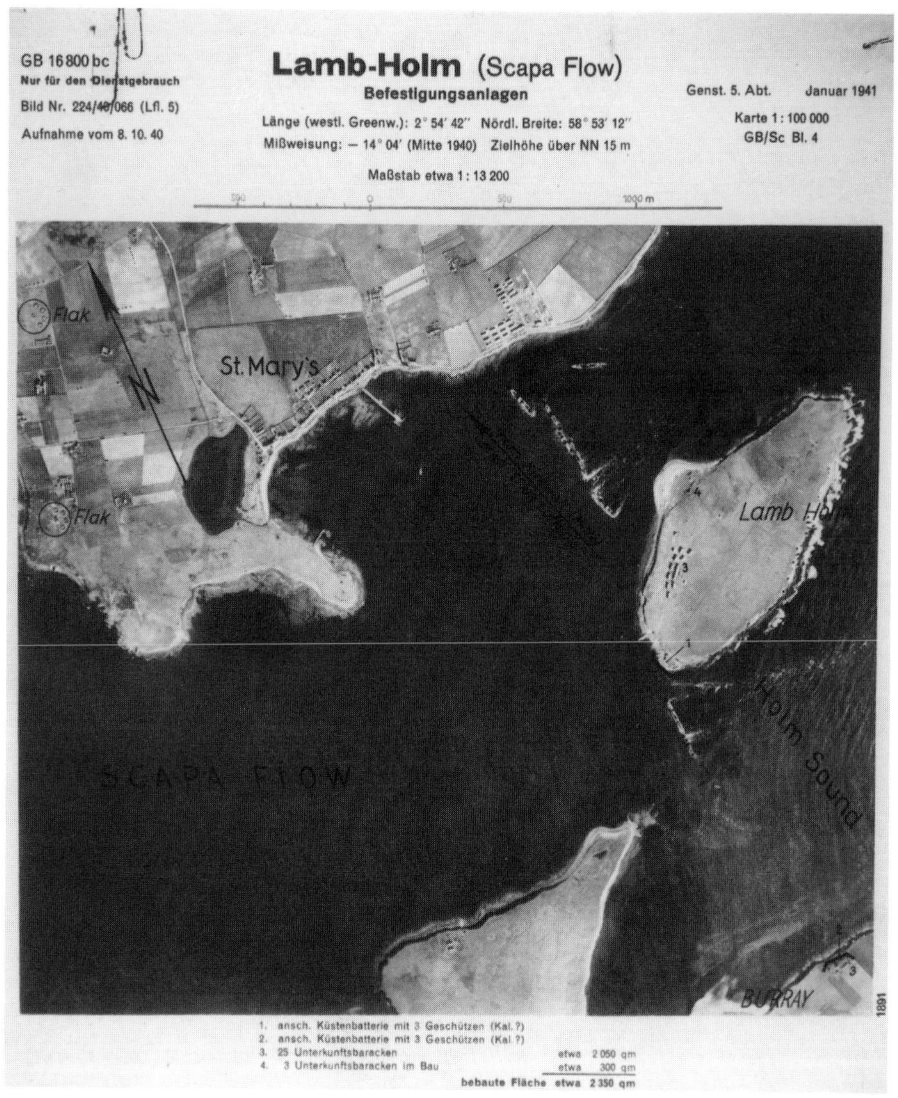

Fig. 121
Luftwaffe reconnaissance picture of the Kirk Sound area, taken on 8 October 1940, almost one year after U-47 *slipped through the screen of blockships between Lamb Holm and the mainland.*

It was not quite the end. A small staff stayed on to look after the installations, and on the morning of 30 March the Union flag of the Admiralty Civil establishment was hoisted in place of the White Ensign. The Royal Navy refuelling station at Lyness continued to replenish visiting ships until 1976, when it was finally closed in a round of defence cuts.

The ownership of the scuttled German ships changed hands a couple of times in the 1970s but there has been no more salvage work and they now constitute a prime attraction for skindivers. In September 1965 the large ships' bells from the *Derfflinger* and the *Friedrich der Grosse* and the former's seal were officially returned to the German navy in a ceremony at Faslane. The bell from the light cruiser *Karlsruhe* was retrieved 'unofficially' by some RAF divers and kept until it too was returned to the present German frigate of the same name

Fig. 122

August 1942. Rubble is being dumped to form the base of the causeway between Burray and Glims Holm, and the tide still flows through gaps in the further section.

in October 1991; the certificate commemorating this event in Kingston-upon-Hull bears the fitting words 'our common naval history'.[93]

At the head of the beach in Scapa Bay there now stands a memorial garden to the *Royal Oak*. Here are listed the names of those who went down with her – twenty-four officers, 786 men, eighteen Maltese ratings serving as stewards and cooks, and five NAAFI staff. A buoy marks where the *Royal Oak* herself lies and every year the navy lays a White Ensign on the slowly decaying wreck. Diving is forbidden on what is classed as an official war grave. At memorial services the men who died here are remembered with wreaths; and surviving members of U-boat crews are invited to join the proceedings. Mass is celebrated

Fig. 123
April 1944. The causeway between Glims Holm and Lamb Holm under construction. The temporary rail line allowed the massive concrete blocks to be run to the foot of the crane which then placed them on the sides of the structure.

monthly in the Italian chapel.

Rusting, barnacle-encrusted hulks of some of the blockships remain beside the Barriers and in Burra Sound. On the west side of the Flow, Lyness has slipped back into a kind of sleepy existence. The scattered farms have made use of some of the service buildings for garages and sheds, and many remain in various states of decay. Tourists come to the shop and the Hoy Hotel on the daily roll-on, roll-off ferry from Houton. The single surviving fuel tank houses an audio-visual presentation of the base's history. The Orkney Islands Council bought the site from the MOD in 1977 and has also turned the pumphouse of the base into a museum to commemorate the wartime activity.

Fig. 124
Some of the Italian POWs formed a dance band.

Fig. 125 (left)
A group of Italian POWs outside the chapel they created from two Nissen huts on the islet of Lamb Holm. The leader of the project, Domenico Chiochetti, is the short man standing on the extreme left.

Fig. 126
HMS King George V.

Lyness is still a bare, bleak place when the wind is in the north, combing through the grass, thistles and wire fences. Up on the brae above the village lies the naval cemetery with the graves of many of the British dead who did not go down with their ships or were buried at sea. This area of trim grass enclosed by a low drystone wall has graves from both Wars, a poignant last anchorage for seamen of all nationalities, with memorial stones for seven German seamen who lost their lives during the scuttling of their Fleet in 1919, as well as for three

Fig. 127
Relief and congratulations for the men of 828 and 841 Squadrons on HMS Implacable *after an air strike on Norway.*

Fig. 128
Pilots of 1771 Squadron on HMS Implacable *in Scapa Flow.*

Muslims, a Parsee and a Buddhist. Across the Firth, on the highest point of Dunnet Head, almost 400 feet above the sea, concrete shells of the wartime observation posts stand as another memorial, filled with the ghosts of the men and women who kept a watch on Scapa Flow.

Fig. 129
HMS Implacable *at anchor in Scapa Flow. One of the largest carriers to serve in the Second World War, the 23,450-ton* Implacable *carried over sixty aircraft and had a speed of thirty-two knots. Commissioned in August 1944, she served at Scapa Flow for only a few months before being posted to the Far East. She was scrapped in 1955.*

Big ships still use the Flow – not battleships but oil tankers, coming to the oil terminal on Flotta. The installations on the island are built more or less on the site occupied all those years ago by the armed services. On a misty day, looking south across the sea, the silhouettes of the waiting tankers catch an echo of how the anchorage might have looked when the dreadnoughts made this place their home.

Fig. 130 (opposite, top) *Wrens march past at Lyness.*

Fig. 131 (opposite, below) *Piles of old hut timbers during the demolition of the Lyness base in 1958.*

Fig. 132 (above) *HMS* Vanguard, *the Royal Navy's last battleship.*

REFERENCES

For a more comprehensive account of the base one can do no better than refer to W.S. Hewison's *This Great Harbour*, now out of print. Gregor Lamb's *Sky over Scapa 1939–1945* is the essential work on aerial operations, and for the story from the viewpoint of the service personnel the collection of reminiscences in *Scapa Flow*, compiled by Malcolm Brown and Patricia Meehan for a BBC documentary in 1968, is invaluable. Details of these and other sources used in this book are given below.

All ADM (Admiralty) references are housed in the Public Record Office, Kew.

1. There are many general accounts of naval history in this period. I have used mainly Howarth (1979), Bennett (1983) and Halpern (1994).
2. ADM 116/1293. 'Scapa Flow defence arrangements 1912–1914'. This collection of documents is the source for most of my information about the plans for Scapa Flow at this time.
3. Graeme Spence's original map is in the National Maritime Museum.
4. ADM 12–155.
5. Hewison provides details of the earlier history of Scapa.
6. *Orcadian*, 17 April 1909.
7. ADM 116/1293.
8. ADM 1/8380/150.
9. Information from Stromness Museum.
10. *Orkney Herald*, 12 August 1914.
11. Roskill (1960) is my main source for naval history during the Second World War.
12. Sutherland Manson. Published in Young.
13. *Inverness Courier*, 14 August 1914.
14. *Orkney Herald*, 15 August 1917.
15. *Inverness Courier*, 14 August 1914.
16. Bacon.
17. Howarth.
18. Halpern.
19. Howarth.
20. Hewison
21. Howarth.
22. Botting.
23. Bennett.
24. Ibid.
25. *John o'Groat Journal*, 4 July 1919, contains the text of Rear-Admiral Grant's after-dinner speech.
26. Bacon.
27. Iain Sutherland.
28. Information from Stromness Museum.
29. Sydney Smith, quoted in Brown and Meehan.
30. Albert Exell, quoted in Brown and Meehan.
31. Halpern.
32. *John o'Groat Journal*, 9 June 1916.
33. W.R. Nisbet, quoted in Brown and Meehan.
34. Information from Stromness Museum.
35. Hoehling.
36. Kemp (1993).
37. H.S.M. Taylor, in the *John o'Groat Journal*, 21 November 1997.
38. Kemp (1998).
39. Churchill, vol. II.

40. Information from Stromness Museum; also Bennett.
41. Liddle.
42. Halpern.
43. Brown and Meehan.
44. *John o'Groat Journal*, 4 July 1919.
45. Information on US Navy ships is from the *Dictionary of American Naval Fighting Ships*, accessed via http://www.uss-salem.org/danfs.
46. Halpern.
47. Howarth. Several books provide accounts of the surrender and last days of the German High Seas Fleet; I have relied on van der Wat.
48. *John o'Groat Journal*, 6 December 1918.
49. George, my main source for the story of the inter-war salvage operations.
50. ADM 116/5790 'History of the Fleet Base: Scapa Flow 1937–1946.' Much of my information about activities in the Flow during the Second World War is drawn from this comprehensive, detailed file.
51. Lamb.
52. *John o'Groat Journal*, 27 January 1939.
53. Bridges.
54. Munro.
55. Vernon Coles, quoted in Arthur.
56. Information from Sir Roderick Macdonald.
57. Information from the Lyness Visitor Centre.
58. Churchill, vol I.
59. There are several accounts of the sinking of the *Royal Oak*. I have relied mainly on Botting, with supplementary material from a translation of Prien's logbook.
60. Information from Sir Roderick Macdonald.
61. Caldwell, quoted in Arthur.
62. Johnston, quoted in Brown and Meehan.
63. The Harrison story is from *John o'Groat Journal*, 20 October 1939.
64. Information from Ella Stephen.
65. *Passing Through*.
66. Munro.
67. Lamb.
68. *John o'Groat Journal*, 20 October 1939.
69. *John o'Groat Journal*, 16 February 1940.
70. Churchill, vol. I.
71. *Highland News*, 23 March 1940.
72. Information from William Mowatt.
73. *Wings over Wick*.
74. Glass.
75. Brown and Meehan.
76. Iris Goody, quoted in Brown and Meehan.
77. Jeanne Frith, quoted in Brown and Meehan.
78. Munro.
79. Paul Smith, quoted in Brown and Meehan.
80. ADM 116/5790.
81. McAra.
82. Churchill, vol. VI.
83. Churchill, vol. IV.
84. Coles, quoted in Arthur.
85. ADM 116/1293.
86. Most of my information on the causeways and the Italian prisoners of war is taken from MacDonald.
87. *Orcadian*, 17 May 1945.
88. Brown and Meehan.
89. *Orcadian*, 5 December 1946.
90. *John o'Groat Journal*, 28 May 1954.
91. *Orcadian*, April 1957.
92. J.N.Walton, quoted in Brown and Meehan.
93. Information about the *Karlsruhe* bell was provided by Noel Donaldson, Wick, and Caroline Hogg, RAF Coningsby.

BIBLIOGRAPHY

Arthur, M., *The Navy: 1939 to the Present*. Hodder & Stoughton, London, 1997.

Bacon, Sir R.H., *The Life of John Rushworth Earl Jellicoe*. Cassell, London, 1936.

Bennett, G., *Naval Battles of the First World War*. Pan, London, 1983.

Botting, D., *The U-Boats*. Time-Life, Amsterdam, 1979.

Bridges, A., *Scapa Ferry*. Davies, London, 1957.

Brown, M. and Meehan, P., *Scapa Flow*. Allen Lane, London, 1968.

Churchill, W.S., *The Second World War* (6 vols). Cassell, London, 1948–54.

Curtis, D., *A Most Secret Squadron*. Skitten Books, Wimborne, 1995.

Falconer, J., *RAF Fighter Airfields of World War 2*. Ian Allan, Shepperton, 1993.

George, S.C., *Jutland to Junkyard*. Patrick Stephen, London, 1973. Pbk edn, Birlinn, Edinburgh, 1999.

Glass, N.M., *Caithness and the War 1939–1945*. North of Scotland Newspapers, Wick, 1948, re-issued 1994.

Goulter, C.J.M., *A Forgotten Offensive: Royal Air Force Coastal Command's Anti-Shipping Campaign 1940–1945*. Frank Cass, London, 1995.

Halpern, P.G., *A Naval History of World War One*. UCL, London, 1994.

Hewison, W.S., *This Great Harbour: Scapa Flow*. Orkney Press, Kirkwall, 1985.

Hoehling, A.A., *The Great War at Sea*. Barker, London, 1965.

Howarth, D., *The Dreadnoughts*. Time-Life, Amsterdam, 1979.

Kemp, P., *Convoy*. Arms & Armour Press, London, 1993.

Kemp, P., *Sea Warfare*. Arms & Armour Press, London, 1998.

Lamb, G., *Sky over Scapa, 1939–1945*. Birsay, Orkney, 1991.

Liddle, P.H., *The Airman's War 1914–18*. Blandford Press, Poole, 1987.

McAra, C., *Mainly in Minesweepers*. Leach, London, 1991.

MacDonald, J., *Churchill's Prisoners: The Italians in Orkney 1942–1944*. Orkney Wireless Museum, Kirkwall, 1987.

Manson, S., 'Some wartime memories of Stroma'. *The Orkney View*. Reprinted in Young, D.A. (ed), *Stroma*. North of Scotland Newspapers, Wick, 1992.

Miller, J., *A Wild and Open Sea*. Orkney Press, Kirkwall, 1994.

Miller, J., *Salt in the Blood*. Canongate, Edinburgh, 1999.

Munro, H., *War Diary 1940–45*. Northern Archive, Wick.

Passing Through. Primary 7, Miller Academy, Thurso, undated.

Roskill, S.W., *The Navy at War 1939–1945*. Collins, London, 1960.

Smith, P.L., *The Naval Wrecks of Scapa Flow*. Orkney Press, Kirkwall, 1989.

Spence, G., *Chart of Scapa Flow, 1812*. NMM G212: 14/5 MS. National Maritime Museum, Greenwich.

Sutherland, I., *From Herring to Seine Net Fishing on the East Coast of Scotland*. Wick, 1985.

van der Wat, D., *The Grand Scuttle: The Sinking of the German Fleet at Scapa Flow in 1919*. Hodder & Stoughton, London, 1982. Re-issued Birlinn, Edinburgh, 1997.

Wings over Wick 1939–1945: a compilation of memories of RAF Wick. Primary 7, Hillhead School, Wick, 1993.